ATTP 4-15 (FM 55-50)

ARMY WATER TRANSPORT OPERATIONS

February 2011

Headquarters, Department of the Army

Published by Books Express Publishing
Books Express Publishing, 2011
ISBN 978-1-78039-982-9

Books Express publications are available from all good retail and online booksellers. For
publishing proposals and direct ordering please contact us at: info@books-express.com

Army Tactics, Techniques, and Procedures
No. 4-15

Headquarters
Department of the Army
Washington, DC, 11 February 2011

Army Water Transport Operations

Contents

Page

Distribution Restriction: This manual is approved for public release. Distribution is unlimited.

*This publication supersedes FM 55-50 dated, 30 September 1993

Preface

The transformation of the Army into a strategically responsive, expeditionary force that is dominant across the full spectrum of operations requires significant cultural, doctrinal and organizational change as well as advanced technological solutions. Such changes and technology must support the Army at every point on the spectrum of operations and must be suitable for the current as well as future forces. These changes and technologies must offer far-reaching capabilities that enable the Capstone Concept for Joint Operations (CCJO) and the Army's Future Force Capstone Concept. Simply improving existing platforms, doctrine, organizations and Army culture does not support the transformation envisioned in either of the aforementioned conceptual documents.

Achieving this robust water transport capability requires new ways and means - enabled by truly transformational doctrine, organizations, training, materiel, leadership and education, personnel and facilities (DOTMLPF) and policy. The major shift in Army watercraft operation focuses on our ability to rapidly project and sustain operational forces within and through the littoral areas of the world. Expeditionary units and enabling technologies provide the commander the water transport capability to achieve positional advantage over operational and tactical distances. These water transport assets are not limited to operating in major or minor ports, but can also operate in austere port environments or over bare beaches. To maximize effectiveness, combat forces must be able to move autonomously, plan and rehearse while en route, and arrive in an immediately employable configuration. Transformation also emphasizes an improved link between operations and logistics, resulting in precise, reliable distributed support and sustainment to the warfighter. Future watercraft, and the units that employ them, must be fast, efficient, and agile; able to move with precision in a quickly changing environment. They must be capable of moving intact current and future force units forward of the strategic port; delivering platforms laden with retail supply; or delivering humanitarian and disaster relief materiel, all the while staying fully aware of the current and future operational situation. Army water transport forces provide the combatant commanders the maneuver capability to rapidly move forces, support and sustainment to the right place, at the right time, and in the right quantities.

As the Army transforms, potential adversaries will adopt anti-access strategies. State or non-state forces will rely on anti-access measures to delay or counter the application of U.S. military capabilities. Future adversaries will marshal their limited assets and focus them on the most likely points of entry into the region. Traditionally, these are major air and seaports or major geographical choke points that must be navigated to achieve entry. Joint Force enabling concepts, units and technologies must provide the operational commander lift assets that bypass these known points, diminishing any asymmetrical advantage held by an adversary. They must allow the commander to pick the time and place of their choosing to initiate action and, thereby, to seize and hold the initiative in a tactical environment. Army watercraft and Army soldier-mariners must be fully trained, equipped and capable of operating in this dynamic joint environment.

Chapters will be updated accordingly as DOD and Army leadership make decisions regarding DOTMLPF and policy that inform further development of ATTP 4-15.

This publication applies to the Active Army, the Army National Guard (ARNG)/Army National Guard of the United States (ARNGUS), and the United States Army Reserve (USAR) unless otherwise stated.

Headquarters, United States Army Training and Doctrine Command(TRADOC), is the proponent for this publication. The preparing agency is the Training and Doctrine Development Directorate, U.S. Army Combined Arms Support Command. Send written comments and recommendations on DA Form 2028 (Recommended Changes to Publications and Blank Forms) to Commander, U.S. Army Combined Arms Support Command, ATTN: ATCL-TDD, 2221 Adams Avenue, Fort Lee, Virginia 23801.

Chapter 1

Army Watercraft: A Joint Power Projection Capability

1-1.   As key platforms for enabling water transport capability to the Joint Force, U.S. Army watercraft directly impact the Nation's ability to employ military instruments of National power. It is within the strategic and joint context that our doctrine is set, and it is within dynamic strategic and joint environments that our watercraft and soldier-mariners operate.

1-2.   As we provide global leadership, universal reach and access boost America's success in executing our National Security Strategy. The Department of Defense is transforming to better meet the broad array of challenges that America may face. Transformation is about providing a wholly different product to meet customers' future needs – in this case, the needs of those who benefit from, and those who carry out the Nation's Security and Defense Strategies. In executing these strategies, we face an increasingly complex joint operating environment described in the Capstone Concept for Joint Operations (CCJO). The CCJO states, "American security and prosperity in a globalized future will be linked inextricably to those of others. The United States will necessarily be a leader Nation to which much of the rest of the world will look for stability and security. It will continue to fall to the United States and its partner nations to protect and sustain the peaceful global system of interdependent networks of trade, finance, information, law and governance. Maintaining freedom of action and access around the globe is as much a requirement for the functioning of this peaceful global system as it is for the conduct of military operations. This will require continuous engagement throughout the world and persistent presence achieved through the forward deployment of U.S. joint forces."

1-3.   The CCJO also identifies another condition that will continue to govern the conduct of U.S. joint operations, i.e., the need to conduct and sustain them at global distances. The CCJO states, "The most likely occasions requiring the commitment of joint forces will arise, as they have for the past half-century, in places where few or no forces are permanently stationed. America's ability to project power rapidly and conduct and sustain operations globally thus will remain critically dependent on air and maritime freedom of movement and on sufficient strategic and operational lift. Future operational success will also rely increasingly on the use of space and cyberspace. Providing adequate lift and maintaining sufficient control of the global "commons" – areas of sea, air, space, and cyberspace that belong to no one state – thus will remain a vital imperative of future joint force design."

1-4.   Within the context of unified action (i.e, employing the diplomatic, informational, military and economic instruments of national power), water transport operations have the most profound impact on military and economic instruments of national power. The following section will focus on the linkage between these two instruments and Army water transport capability.

INFLUENCE OF WATER TRANSPORT ON INSTRUMENTS OF NATIONAL POWER

1-5.   Commercial ocean transit and commercial enterprises in the littorals and coastal areas of the world are absolutely crucial to the economic aspect of our security strategy. We must have an unmatched capability to operate militarily, in these domains.

1-6.   Army water transport forces and assets provide operational maneuver and distributed support and sustainment capability at the confluence of the land and sea domains; they can also extend operations within the land domain, using inland waterways and navigable rivers.

1-7.   Furthermore, given the demographics and the centers of global military and economic power, coupled with future population and economic growth factors, access and the ease with which we can transition capability between off-shore (sea) and on-shore (land) domains becomes more and more important to setting conditions for success and enabling our national security. The concentration of global wealth as measured by gross national product occurs primarily in coastal regions, although concentrations of wealth also occur in some inland areas (especially in the United States and Europe). There are also considerable physical risks associated with living in some coastal areas; low-lying atolls, for example, are at risk of catastrophic events such as hurricanes, cyclones, tsunamis, and storm surge flooding, as well as losses incurred from both sudden and chronic shoreline erosion.

1-8.   Army watercraft missions, aimed at evacuating people threatened by natural disasters, mitigating loss of life and infrastructure damage, introducing first responders and law-enforcement capability, help to mitigate the economic impacts of such events in the most critical economic portions of the world. They also demonstrate a steadfast commitment by the United States which ties directly to information and diplomacy as instruments of national power. Additionally, water transport operations in response to Weapons of Mass Destruction (WMD) threats and/or attacks or natural disasters here in the United States could be crucial.

1-9.   History has taught us the value of a robust water transport capability underpinning military operations. Rapid, global, water transport response capability continues as a vital military instrument of national power. As we focus on the "traditional" threat challenge areas, Army watercraft's role becomes the precise, surgical introduction of combat power and the continued sustainment of the force – enabling options across the operational themes from peacetime military engagement to major combat operations.

THE FOUR STRATEGIC THREAT CHALLENGE AREAS

1-10. The National Security Strategy (NSS), National Defense Strategy (NDS) and Quadrennial Defense Review (QDR) discuss four threat areas: Traditional, Irregular, Catastrophic and Disruptive. The Department is transforming to better balance its capabilities across four categories of challenges.

1-11. The graphic portrayal and the risk considerations associated with the strategic threat challenge areas are noted in Figure 1-1. Also worthy of note is the confluence of these strategic challenges with order of effect implications for the capabilities that the U.S. should develop.

Irregular
(U) Challenges arising from the adoption or employment of unconventional methods; terrorism, insurgency, civil war, etc.

(U) Examples: Unconventional techniques employed by enemy forces – Suicide high-speed surface boats

Catastrophic
(U) Potential WMD threats to US Forces conducting tactical movements in a theater of operations

(U) Examples: Nuclear or chemical weapons employed by state actors and/or terrorist organizations

Higher

LIKELIHOOD

Lower

VULNERABILITY

Higher

Traditional
(U) Challenges posed by States employing legacy and advanced military capabilities and recognizable military forces

(U) Examples: Conventional weapons employed by enemy forces – mines, small caliber shore-based weapons fire

Disruptive
(U) Competitors employing breakthrough technologies to supplant our advantages

(U) Examples: Use of trained marine mammals to deliver explosive loads against VSB

Lower

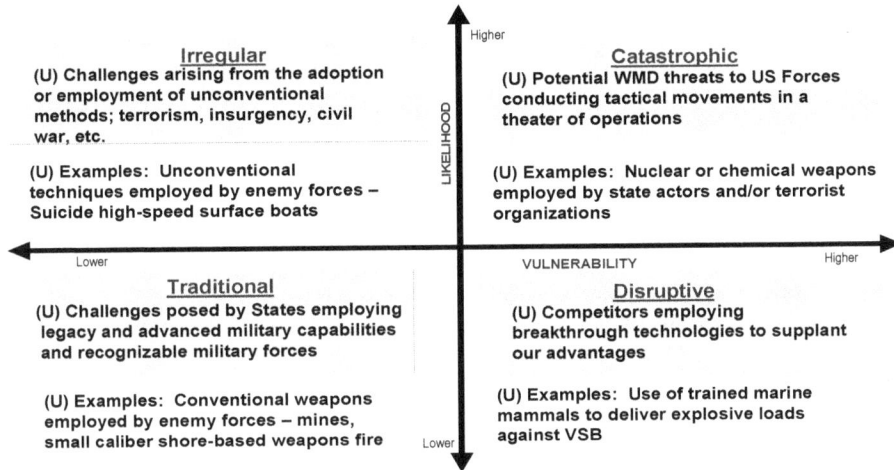

Figure 1-1. Threat Challenge—Risk Horizon

1-12. Clearly water transport maneuver and sustainment capability plays a key role across all four threat challenge areas. It provides a course of action to introduce combat power through improved or austere *points of debarkation*; to insert, sustain and retract special operators; to rapidly deploy and employ tailored multi-national peacekeeping forces; to introduce first responders, including chemical, biological, radiological, and nuclear (CBRN) assessment teams to deliver medical/humanitarian relief supplies; to evacuate threatened populations and other roles/missions limited only by the imagination of the planners and operators.

1-13. The strategic sealift and intratheater lift by Army watercraft provide the responsiveness envisioned by the nations leadership and the ability to operate within the decision cycles of astute and dynamic adversaries. The capability to rapidly deploy Army watercraft into theater for operational and tactical maneuver in the littorals, coupled with sustainment of land combat power are key enablers for our integrated global posture and basing strategy.

1-14. As an extension of the land domain, Army water transport maneuver and distributed sustainment capability blurs the traditional lines between the Navy, Military Sealift Command, US Transportation Command (USTRANSCOM) and the joint force commander. Command relationships and roles/missions for Army water transport operations are, and must continue to be, highly adaptable and easily transition between varying mission types.

1-15. Army water transport assets provide capability for underpinning how the future, expeditionary joint force projects and sustains combat power, from peacetime military engagement to major combat operations.

ESTABLISHING AND VALIDATING JOINT REQUIREMENTS

1-16. Water transport operations by the Army watercraft fleet and its enablers provide a critical capability at all levels and across operational themes from peacetime military engagement to major combat operations and joint capability areas. Water transport primarily support the logistics JCA at the Tier 1 level, deployment and distribution at the Tier 2 level, and move/sustain the force at the Tier 3 level.

1-17. Active engagement at all levels in the Joint Capabilities Integration and Development System (JCIDS) process and venues, to inform the Joint community on "the ability to" implications of Army water transport operations, can not be over emphasized. Water transport Proponency, through the appropriate Functional Capability Boards and the JCA Roadmaps will help to ensure informed decisions are made for leveraging a heretofore underutilized physical domain.

SUMMARY

1-18. Maneuver in the littorals is the essence of the capability that Army Watercraft bring to Geographic Combatant Commanders (GCC) and Joint Force Commanders, which may take place in one or more of our Nation's four challenge areas. The Army watercraft community is poised to rapidly introduce and sustain operationally significant combat power anywhere on the globe. Army Watercraft will play a crucial role in realizing a robust water transport capability to provide operational maneuver across land and sea domains for combatant commanders.

Chapter 2

Watercraft Platforms, Organizations, Training, and Personnel

The purpose of this chapter is to describe the Army watercraft fleet and other capabilities in terms of the total requirement, missions, capabilities, distribution, and modernization goals. It introduces and graphically portrays individual vessels that make up the Army watercraft fleet. It addresses vessel mission, transportability, characteristics and capabilities, vessel requirements, on-hand quantities, procurement or divestiture actions, distribution, and specific or ongoing actions required for the particular vessel. The tables for each vessel provide a synopsis of Army watercraft requirements that shape the fleet.

ORGANIZATION AND CAPABILITIES

ORGANIZATIONAL DESCRIPTION

2-1. The Logistics Support Vessels and JHSV, detachments each consist of one vessel, its assigned crew and unit equipment is designed to be self-sustaining over extended periods. They are normally attached to an Army transportation terminal battalion, but are equipped to integrate with joint land and maritime forces as well.

2-2. Smaller vessels, such as landing craft and tugs, are organized into companies and detachments, with multiple vessels, assigned crews, support personnel and unit equipment. The unit deploys several vessels, with support elements from the unit headquarters detachment to conduct operations. Large scale missions may require multiple units to cover the full spectrum of water transport tasks required to support brigade combat teams in synchronized operations. These companies and detachments are normally attached to an Army transportation terminal battalion for command and control during operations.

2-3. **Operational Description** Vessels are employed to move, maneuver, and reposition personnel, cargo, and equipment.

- **Mission:** To perform waterborne transportation of personnel, cargo, equipment and sustainment forward of the strategic port, including fully operational combat teams or provide lift of outsized equipment into littorals and austere environments.

- **Assignment:** Vessels are globally-responsive theater assets, designed to support operational and tactical maneuver, support and sustainment of joint forces. They can support any level of joint or coalition force operations, but will normally be assigned to the theater sustainment command, with further attachment to a sustainment brigade or a transportation terminal battalion.

- **Capabilities:** The larger, faster vessels provide operational maneuver and repositioning of forces during intra-theater lift, waterborne tactical and joint amphibious or riverine operations. Smaller landing craft does the same tasks, but with smaller cargo loads. The large, ocean-going tug and its smaller counterpart provide significant towing, salvage, ship-assist, recovery and port operations capability to terminal operations. These vessels are designed to support the full spectrum of military operations by providing the joint force commander with the ability to bypass degraded lines of communications, such as highway main supply routes (MSR), and conduct tactical operations from off-shore and through inland waterways.

- **Mobility:** All vessels require a sufficient number of qualified personnel and authorized equipment and supplies to self-deploy or conduct continuous operations in a theater of operations.

- **Personnel:** Watercraft units are organized to operate on an around-the-clock basis over extended operational periods in various weather conditions and threat environments. Designed to operate as a part of the future, modular Army that will operate as part of an expeditionary and campaign-quality Joint Force, Army watercraft are organized with warrant officers and enlisted personnel assigned as crew according to size of vessel and mission set. Numbers and MOS of personnel assigned will differ due to each vessel's class, mission, and size.

2-4.   The crew consists of personnel assigned to the deck or engine departments who perform tasks as directed by the officers aboard in their respective department. These duties can include underway watch, operating ship's equipment, cargo stowage planning, upload and discharge operations, flight operations, ship security, and routine cleaning and maintenance of the ship and the equipment on deck, in the engine room, and in the galley. Crewing requirements for individual platform types are found in Appendix D.

WATERCRAFT CAPABILITY DESCRIPTION

2-5.   **Vessel Performance** Army watercraft deploy worldwide and are capable of supporting operational movement, and force repositioning, as well as distribution and sustainment in various roles, including: deployment from staging bases to insertion points in Joint Operation Areas (JOA), Joint Logistics over the Shore (JLOTS) and single service LOTS, extending the intra-theater mobility of combat equipment and increasing the capability to distribute equipment and supplies across the entire spectrum of operational themes from peacetime military engagement to major combat operations.

2-6.   **Core Competencies** To enable the Combatant Commander to meet land maneuver requirements, Army Watercraft possess the following core competencies:

- Intra-theater Lift - Army watercraft are designed to perform missions specifically related to intra-theater movement of combat power and sustainment. While capable of deploying over strategic distances, Army watercraft are not strategic lift platforms, but are a critical link between strategic lift and land-oriented tactical maneuver operations. This capability provides the Joint Forces Commander (JFC) the flexibility to tactically position and support the Joint operational scheme of maneuver, with unprecedented speed and magnitude.

- Logistics over the Shore – Lighters transport cargo from ship to shore or Seabase to shore, reducing operational footprint ashore and provide an alternative to using piers and austere ports.

- Anti-Access/Port Denial – Circumvent enemy anti-access strategies by providing alternative water transport means for achieving combat power throughput when strategic and tactical ports are unavailable.

- Surface Infiltration – Army watercraft are distinctly suitable as secure "mother ship" staging bases for various types of special operations infiltration/exfiltration operations. (FM 3-05.212 addresses incorporation of Army watercraft for special operations mission support).

KEY OPERATIONAL CHARACTERISTICS:

Expeditionary Much of the time and resources required today for reception, staging and onward movement will be reduced or eliminated when forces move in combat-ready force packages aboard Army watercraft. Watercraft flexibility complements land maneuver forces' inherent speed and agility by allowing forces to be positioned close to the objective, but out of direct contact with enemy resistance. Further, the Command, Control, Communications, Computers, Intelligence, Surveillance, and Reconnaissance (C4ISR) capability on board vessels enhances maneuver units situational awareness while on the move and provides the capability to conduct mission planning and rehearsal while en route to the objective.

Austere Access. The Army's landing craft are specifically designed to dramatically increase the ability to access points on the littorals that are currently unavailable to Land Maneuver Forces. The vessels' shallow draft, adaptable cargo space and ramp support delivery of intact ground combat units and follow-on support and sustainment at a wide variety of points without the need for improved ports facilities and the added footprint of terminal service operators.

Survivable. Army vessels are capable of operating and surviving in various sea states and adverse weather conditions. Intra-theater sealift movement of units, equipment, and sustainment may require voyages of significant distances, requiring the vessels to not only operate but provide adequate survivability to ensure embarked combat forces arrive ready to conduct operations.

Minimal Footprint. Army watercraft enables the Joint Force to operate at the place and time of its own choosing, regardless of enemy intent, infrastructure or regional political conditions constraining U.S. access. watercraft significantly expand on current lift capabilities with increased speed, survivability, integrated passenger transport, and self-sustaining cargo handling capability.

Stand-Off Capability. Stand-off capability is the ability of the land maneuver commander to conduct logistics and support operations at a relatively safe location distant from the operational area or objective. Army watercraft deliver personnel and operational equipment, enabling land maneuver forces to conduct rapid tactical movement into the operational area. The speed and range of the complement of Army watercraft enables the commander to introduce forces and sustainment using multiple entry points even in reduced access and infrastructure conditions.

Self-Sustaining. Army watercraft's self-sustaining capability is a critical element that increases speed, enables expeditionary operations and reduces the logistics footprint in the operational environment.

Network Interoperability. Army vessels incorporate joint, interoperable C4ISR capability, fully integrated with the Common Operational Picture (COP). This allows them to maintain situational awareness and conduct battle command on the move (BCOTM). JHSVs can also provide embarked forces with real-time connectivity to their command and control structure, and situational awareness of the common operational picture enabling ground combat Commanders to avoid information blackouts while maneuvering. Embarked forces can conduct mission planning and rehearsal while en route.

Global Reach. The fleet possesses global reach capability The larger vessels are designed to be forward-deployed, providing continuous operational support to a wide variety of missions, to include peacekeeping operations, disaster relief, non-combatant evacuation operations, support to the theater support and cooperation program (TSCP), as well as priority support and sustainment operations. Other watercraft lift capabilities are forward-stationed in operational units or prepositioned stock for ready availability to combatant commanders.

Joint Interoperability. Although designed to support simultaneous deployment, employment and sustainment of tactical ground maneuver forces, Army vessels are capable of supporting a wide range of Joint, interagency and multi-national operations. With the JHSV, the fleet is capable of supporting aviation operations, small craft and unmanned craft operations, and provide adequate on-board auxiliary power, network, water and compressed air to support a variety of mission-specific equipment or modules.

Security and Protection. Army watercraft are not designed as naval combatant craft and are not intended for offensive operations in direct contact with enemy forces. However, in its role as a tactical movement and support platform, watercraft support the enhanced lethality of land maneuver forces by providing speed and agility to enter and leave an objective area, circumventing anti-access strategies by using waterways as maneuver and supply routes, and realize surprise in the conduct of decisive operations. Army watercraft will therefore operate in the uncertain threat environment described in the JOE and are equipped with the ability to defend and protect crew, cargo and embarked passengers, to include various capabilities to detect and defend against surface (land and water) and air based threats with lethal and non-lethal means.

Autonomy and Sustainment. Army watercraft are capable of operating alone or in conjunction with other vessels. The large vessels operate as a typical separate detachment or company, planning and coordinating external support as required from normal Army, Joint and commercial resources. Support is coordinated for large tugs and smaller vessels through unit headquarters and Liaison Officers.

Command Relationships. Army watercraft are organized to operate within the command, control, and communications architecture of a Joint and expeditionary modular force. The following paragraphs describe how - and where – Army watercraft operate.

CATEGORIES OF WATERCRAFT

2-7.   Watercraft fall into three categories: high-speed vessels, lighters, and floating utility craft. These three categories are defined according to the missions they perform.

2-8.   High-speed vessels are designed to provide high speed operational movement of intact ready-to-fight unit sets within a theater of operation. Designed to operate independently, high-speed vessels such as the JHSV vessel provide intratheater lift between an offshore intermodal sustainment base and littoral battlefield, within the littoral battlefield or along rivers within the area of operations (AO).

2-9.   Lighters are used to conduct heavy sustainment lift, transporting outsized equipment, lighterage (cargo), and personnel between ships, from ship to shore, or for intra-theater transport. Lighters are further classified into conventional displacement (landing craft) or modular causeway systems (powered ferry). Army lighters include the Logistic Support Vessel (LSV), Landing Craft Utility (LCU), Landing Craft Mechanized (LCM) and the Causeway Ferry.

2-10. Floating utility craft perform operations incidental to water terminal operations, except lighterage service. Watercraft in this category are harbor and oceangoing tugs, pusher tugs, floating cranes, barges, floating causeways, roll-on/roll-off discharge facilities, and modular/side-loadable warping tugs.

VESSEL CLASSES

Army watercraft fall into one of three vessel classes (A, B and C):

- **Class A - Vessels Designed for Continuous Operation.** This class includes the large high speed vessels, Large Tugboats, Logistics Support Vessel, and Landing Craft Utility (LCU-2000). These vessels have numerous critical subsystems (such as propulsion, electrical power generation, environmental control, navigation/communications, and firefighting) which demand constant attention. These vessels are capable of long duration, independent mission profiles; some of them are capable of independent ocean crossing voyages. These vessels must be crewed for 24 hour-per-day operations using watch standing techniques and procedures. Within this class of vessels are two sub-classes. They are:

  - A1 - normally operated in coastal waters.

  - A2 - fully ocean capable.

Masters and chief engineers on all A1 vessels stand a normal underway watch and remain on call during off-duty hours. On class A2 vessels, the master and chief engineer are not part of the watch standing rotation, but remain on call 24 hours a day.

- **Class B - Self-propelled Vessels Designed for Intermittent Use or for Relatively Continuous Use in Localized Areas.** This class includes small tugs (ST), smaller landing craft (LCM-8) and all causeway ferry systems. Because they generally operate in confined areas such as harbors or at Logistics-over-the-Shore (LOTS) sites, they typically have significant shore-side support. Their onboard subsystems are less complex than those of the larger vessels. Crewing for this type vessel generally is shift oriented and two separate crews are required for 24 hour operations.

- **Class C - Non-self-propelled Watercraft.** This class includes all barges. The crew requirements vary widely with the purpose and design of the barge. Regardless of their specific function, they are usually subject to wind, tide, and, sea state. When afloat, they have a constant requirement for tending, even when not being actively employed for their designed purpose. Except for the floating crane noted above, crewing for these vessels is generally shift oriented. There is one type of non-self-propelled watercraft in this category. The barge derrick crane, except for lack of propulsion subsystems, meets all the requirements for watch standing crew. Although this vessel is a barge, it has substantial power generation, communications, environmental control, and firefighting subsystems requiring constant attention. It also has live-aboard capability for its crew. This vessel must be crewed for 24 hour-per-day operations using watch standing techniques and procedures.

2-11. Watercraft are fully crewed regardless of the class type vessel. No watercraft can safely operate without a full crew. Generally, fractional crewmembers (such as one marine engineman for two vessels) will not work in watercraft units as the individual craft, even those operating in the same harbor do not necessarily operate in close proximity to each other, and may operate at the same time.

CORE ARMY WATERCRAFT MISSIONS

2-12. Army watercraft platforms do the heavy lifting associated with water transport operational maneuver and the intra-theater sealift of units, equipment and supplies. They support marine terminal and sea-based operations to conduct force closure and to execute distributed support and sustainment of employed forces. Operating as part of the Joint Force, these watercraft and the organizations to which they belong, provide critical capability in mitigating an adversaries anti-access strategy and in overcoming area denial challenges present in the theater of operations. These platforms are organized into the following Army organizations:

- Joint High Speed Vessel Detachment (JHSV).
- Transportation Medium Boat Detachment (LCM-8).
- Transportation Heavy Boat Company (LCU-2000).
- Transportation Modular Causeway Company (ferry, RRDF, floating piers).
- Transportation Floating Craft Company (Tug, barges, floating cranes).
- Logistics Support Vessel Detachment (LSV).
- Transportation Harbormaster Detachment (HMO).

2-13. The following sections (by vessel type) provide the organizational information, current system mission, assessment, capabilities and characteristics, distribution, modernization, and the actions to meet current and future requirements and goals. In order to accurately interpret the contents of this section, the reader must understand the scope of each paragraph as defined:

- Capability—the operational mission of the vessel.
- Transportability—the methods available to transport the vessel to the area of operation.
- Characteristics/capabilities—vessel dimensions; payload in terms of capacity, equipment, and container carrying equivalents; operating range in nautical miles (NM); crew size; and age of craft.
- Length overall—the total length of the vessel in feet.
- Beam—the extreme width of the vessel in feet.
- Displacement—the weight of the total amount of water in long tons that a vessel displaces when afloat (Displacement [light] is the weight stated with no stores, fuel, water, or equipment [basic issue items] aboard. Displacement [loaded] is the weight stated with full stores, fuel, water, and equipment aboard.).

- Deck area—the total square footage of deck space available for loading equipment. It is stated in square footage and, where appropriate, in terms of M1 main battle tanks, Strykers, and 20-foot containers.

- Payload—the total weight a vessel can carry in tons.

- Range—the distance a vessel can travel with one full load of fuel (stated in both light [no cargo] and loaded [fully laden] terms.).

- Draft—the amount of hull underwater in feet when the vessel is afloat (stated in both light (no cargo) and loaded (fully laden) terms).

- Crew size—derived from doctrinally documented requirements, approved changes, additional documentation by HQDA since that change was published, and proponent-advised additional requirements.

- On-hand—the total number of craft on hand.

- Distribution table—Modified TOE (by component) and pre-positioning distribution requirements.

ARMY WATERCRAFT ORGANIZATIONS

JOINT HIGH SPEED VESSEL DETACHMENT (TOE 55888F000)

Mission. To perform high-speed transportation of personnel, cargo, and equipment, including fully operational combat teams, during intra-theater lift, water transport tactical and joint amphibious or riverine operations.

Assignment. To a Theater Sustainment Command, with a sustainment brigade.

Employment. The high speed vessel capability supports the full spectrum of military operations by providing the Combatant Commander with the ability to rapidly bypass degraded lines of communication, shorten MSRs, and conduct tactical operations from offshore and remote bases. It supports the Combatant Commander's ability to build and sustain combat power by giving combat teams the capability to conduct enroute planning and rehearsal while gaining a wide variety of access points in remote and austere theaters of operation.

Capabilities.

- Self-sustainment for a extended periods with accommodations for the crew.

- Transports 700 STONs of unit equipment or sustainment supplies, and 312 combat equipped troops in a single lift.

- Level I combat health and food service support.

- Self-deploy to a theater of operations and meet prescribed equipment requirements to transit the Panama and Suez Canals.

- Capable of underway refueling and vertical replenishment.

- Self protection with crew-served weapons, aviation deck for landing/takeoff of helicopters up to CH-53.

This unit is dependent on:

- Appropriate elements of the supporting units for religious, Echelons II and III combat health support, finance, and personnel and administrative services.

- Transportation Watercraft Maintenance Company or contract MWT support, for field and sustainment maintenance.

- Transportation Harbormaster Detachment, for watercraft operational support.

- Harbor facilities, or the U.S. Navy for refueling.

NSN: Under development
LIN: Z27774

Figure 2-1. Joint High Speed Vessel

Mission: The Joint High Speed Vessel is the Army's next-generation self-deploying watercraft (the Army's documented organization for this craft is the Theater Support Vessel detachment). The JHSV will be faster and possess greater survivability than current generation watercraft. The JHSV will maximize intra-theater lift from an offshore Seabase and rivers to provide the warfighter the capability to operationally move and rapidly maneuver combat ready forces into the forward areas and to provide follow-on sustainment through minor, austere, and degraded ports. This craft requires a pier, quay or causeway for cargo operations. The JHSV is a high-speed operational maneuver capability, complementing a balanced fleet based on adequate high-speed maneuver and lighterage capability.

Transportability: The JHSV is self-deployable anywhere in the world.

Characteristics/capabilities: Following are the expected characteristics of the JHSV:

    Class: A2

    Length overall: Less than103m/338ft

    Beam: Less than 28.5m/93.5ft

    Displacement (weight): 2,359 LT full load

    Deck area: 20,053 square feet (2043.9sq m), with overhead clearance 15'6" (4.8m)

    Payload: 700 short tons (635metric tonnes)

(includes CH-53 on flight deck and 312 combat-loaded troops)

Range:
Light: 4700 NM at 24+ knots
Loaded: 1200 NM at 35+ knots with 600 tons of cargo
Capable of underway refueling

Draft:
10.04ft/3.06 Light
12.57ft/3.83 Loaded

Crew size: 31

On-hand: Distribution and stationing of the JHSV is currently under development pending resolution of procurement strategies. Expectation is the first vessels will be forward-stationed for combatant command responsiveness.

LOGISTICS SUPPORT VESSEL DETACHMENT, (TOE 55530CJ00)

Mission. To provide transportation for vehicles containers, and/or general cargo to remote, underdeveloped areas along coastlines and inland waterways; to support unit deployments, relocations, and port to port operations; to assist in discharging and back-loading ships in a RO/RO or LOTS operation; and provide cargo transportation along coastal main supply routes (MSRs).

Assignment. To a Sustainment Brigade, responsible for port and watercraft operations; normally attached to a Transportation Terminal Battalion.

Capabilities. This team:

- Is capable of self-sustainment for extended periods days with accommodations for a 31-member crew.
- Transports 2,000 STONs of cargo, consisting of vehicles, containers, and/or general cargo.
- Receives and discharges cargo through a bow ramp or stern ramp.
- Beaches with a 1:30 offshore beach gradient with a maximum of 900 STONs of cargo.
- Performs unit maintenance on all organic equipment, except communication, electronic, and navigation (CEN)/C4I equipment.
- Provides combat health service and food service support.
- Is capable of self-deploy to a theater of operations and meets the requirements to transit the Panama and Suez Canals.
- Is dependent on the TOE unit to which assigned or attached for religious, legal, finance, transportation, personnel and administrative services, and logistical support.
- Individuals of these teams can assist in the coordinated defense of the port or terminal.

CRAFT: LOGISTICS SUPPORT VESSEL (LSV)

NSN: 1915-01-153-8801 (LSV1 through 6), 1915-01-495-0036 (LSV 7 and 8)
LIN: V00426

Figure 2-2. Logistics Support Vessel

Mission: The LSV provides worldwide transport of combat vehicles and sustainment cargo. It provides intra-theater line haul of large quantities of cargo and equipment. Tactical resupply missions can be performed to remote underdeveloped coastlines and inland waterways. It is also ideally suited for the discharge or back load of sealift, including Roll-On/Roll-Off (RO/RO) vessels, such as a large medium-speed RO/RO (LMSR). The LSV can transport cargo from ship to shore in Logistics-Over-the-Shore (LOTS) operations, including those in remote areas with unimproved beaches. All container and bulk cargo, tracked and wheeled vehicles, including main battle tanks, dozers, and container-handling equipment, can be transported in LOTS operations. The LSV has both bow and stern ramps for RO/RO cargo, and a bow thruster to conduct beaching, beach extraction, docking and undocking without tug assist. It can also be used for unit deployment and relocation. Because of its shallow draft, the LSV can carry cargo from deep-draft ships to shore ports or areas too shallow for larger ships. The LSV can also execute cargo operations along coastal Lines of Communication (LOC).

Transportability: The LSV can self-deploy anywhere in the world.

Characteristics/capabilities

> **Class:** A2

> **Length overall:** LSV 1 through 6 - 272.75 feet (83.1m); LSV 7 and 8 – 314 feet (95.7m)

> **Beam:** 60 feet (18.3m)

> **Displacement** (loaded): LSV 1 through 6 - 4,199 long tons; LSV 7 & 8 – 5,905 long tons

Deck area: 10,500 sq. ft. (up to 24 M1 main battle tanks or 24 [48 double stacked] 20-foot ISO containers) (975.5 sq meters)

> **Payload:** 2,000 short tons (equivalent payload capacity of 40 C-17s) (1814.4 metric tonnes)

Range: LSV 1 through 6 - Light: 8,200 NM at 11.5 knots, Loaded: 6,500 NM at 11 knots; LSV 7 & 8 – Loaded: 5500 nm at 12 knots

> **Draft:**
> Light: 6 feet (1.8m)
> Loaded: LSV 1 through 6 - 12 feet (3.7m); LSV 7 & 8 – 13 feet

Crew size: 31 (8 warrant officers and 23 enlisted for 24-hour operation)

On-hand: 8

TRANSPORTATION HEAVY WATERCRAFT COMPANY (TOE 55829L000)

Mission. To perform waterborne transportation of personnel, cargo and equipment during intra-theater lift, water terminal and joint amphibious, riverine or logistics-over-the-shore (JLOTS) operations.

Assignment. To a Sustainment Brigade, responsible for port and watercraft operations; normally attached to a Transportation Terminal Battalion.

Employment. Normally, the Transportation Heavy Watercraft Company will be employed in a water terminal, waterborne tactical operation, or joint logistics over-the-shore (JLOTS) operations. It may be attached to the Navy to support joint amphibious operations. It may also operate separately under an appropriate commander, such as a Theater Sustainment Command, in an independent logistics support area.

Capabilities. Based on 75 percent of Landing Craft Utility (LCU) available to operate on a 24-hour basis, this unit is capable of:

- Transporting 1,600 short tons (STONs) of non-containerized cargo. Each vessel makes one trip daily.

- Transporting 288 containers. Each vessel makes 7.2 trips daily.

- Transporting 3,200 combat-equipped personnel. Each vessel makes one trip daily.

- Individuals of this organization can assist in the coordinated defense of the unit's area or installation.

This unit performs unit level maintenance on all organic equipment except CEN/C4I.

This unit is dependent on:

- Appropriate elements of the Army Service Component Command for force health protection, finance, personnel and administrative services, and supplemental transportation support.

- HHC, Transportation Battalion, for religious, legal, field feeding facilities and supervision for assigned cooks who support shore based personnel.

- Seaport Operations Company or supporting unit for automotive maintenance support.

- This unit can support the Heavy Dive Team, and the Light Dive Team, engaged in underwater maintenance support to the Transportation Watercraft Maintenance Company, when METT-TC dictates the use of the Landing Craft, Utility (LCU) as a dive platform.

Craft: Landing Craft, Utility 2000 (LCU-2000)

NSN: 1905-01-154-1191
LIN: L36989

Figure 2-3. Landing Craft, Utility 2000

Mission: The LCU-2000 provides transport of combat vehicles and sustainment cargo. It provides intra-theater movement of cargo and equipment. Tactical resupply missions can be performed to remote, underdeveloped coastlines and inland waterways. This includes missions in LOTS operations in remote areas with austere shore facilities or unimproved beaches. It is also ideally suited for the discharge or back load of sealift, including RO/RO vessels such as an LMSR. All tracked and wheeled vehicles, including main battle tanks, dozers, and container-handling equipment, can be transported in LOTS operations. The LCU-2000 has a bow ramp for RO/RO cargo, and a bow thruster to assist in beaching and beach extraction. It can also be used for deployment and relocation of unit equipment. Because of its shallow draft, the LCU-2000 can carry cargo from deep-draft ships to shore ports or areas too shallow for larger strategic lift ships. These vessels execute cargo operations along coastal LOC.

Transportability: Depending upon distance, weather, sea conditions, and crew training, the LCU-2000 can be self-deployed. It can also be transported aboard a float-on/float-off (FLO/FLO) or lift-on/lift-off (LO/LO) ship. In the case of self-deployment, it has a range (without refueling) of 4,500 miles.

Characteristics/capabilities

Class: A1

Length overall: 174 feet (53m)

Beam: 42 feet (12.8m)

Displacement (weight): 575 long tons (light); 1,087 long tons (loaded)

Deck area: 2,500 sq. ft. (5 M1 main battle tanks or 15 [30 double stacked] 20-foot ISO containers) (232.3 sq meters)

Payload: 350 tons (equivalent payload capacity of 7 C-17 loads) (317.5 metric tonnes)

Range:
Light: 4,500 NM at 12 knots
Loaded: 4,500 NM at 10 knots

Draft:

Light: 8 feet (2.4m)
Loaded: 9 feet (2.7m)

Crew size: 13 (2 warrant officers and 11 enlisted for 24-hour operation)

On-hand: 34

Craft: Landing Craft, Mechanized 8 (LCM-8 Mod 1)

NSN: 1905-00-935-6057 (MOD 1); 1905-01-284-2647 (MOD 0 w/ MOD 1 SLEP) & 1905-01-284-2649
LIN: L36739 (MOD 1); L36767 (MOD 0 with MOD 1 SLEP)

Figure 2-4. Landing Craft, Mechanized 8, Modification 1

Mission: The LCM-8 transports cargo, troops, and vehicles from ship to shore or in retrograde movements. It is also utilized in lighterage and utility work in harbors. It is designed for use in rough or exposed waters and is capable of operating through breakers and grounding on a beach. The bow ramp permits RO/RO operations with wheeled and tracked vehicles. Its small size facilitates its use in confined areas.

Transportability: The LCM-8 can be deck loaded on LSVs, LCU-2000s, commercial bulk carriers, heavy lift ships, and tactical auxiliary crane ships or carried in the well deck of LSDs and LPDs.

Characteristics/capabilities

Class: B

Length overall: 74 feet (22.5m)

Beam: 21 feet (6.4m)

Displacement (weight): 58 long tons (light); 111 long tons (loaded)

Deck area: 620 sq. ft. (two 20-foot ISO containers or 200 combat-equipped soldiers) (57.6 sq meters)

Payload: 53 tons (equivalent payload capacity of one C-17 load) (48 metric tonnes)

Range:
Light: 332 NM at 11 knots
Loaded: 271 NM at 9 knots

Draft:

Light: 3.5 feet (1m)
Loaded: 5 feet (1.5m)

Crew size: 6 enlisted (3 per shift for 24-hour operation)

On-hand: 42

Craft: Landing Craft, Mechanized 8, Modification 2 (LCM-8 MOD 2)

NSN: 1905-01-465-7599
LIN: L36654

Figure 2-5. Landing Craft, Mechanized 8, Modification 2

Mission: The primary mission of the LCM-8 (MOD 2) is command and control (C2), personnel transfer, and light salvage. It is used in harbors and inland waterways. The LCM-8 (MOD 2) is a versatile vessel capable of performing many support functions in conditions up to Sea State 3. As a C2 platform, the LCM-8 (MOD 2) provides the critical link between ship and shore operation centers. It transports Army stevedores between shore points and a ship in a protected environment. It may also be used as a medical evacuation vessel, diver support platform, and firefighting and light salvage boat. The LCM-8 (MOD 2) can work in shallow inlets and rivers as well as retain its original ability to land on an unimproved beach.

Transportability: The LCM-8 (MOD 2) may be deck loaded onto a larger vessel for deployment to overseas locations.

Characteristics/capabilities

Class: B

Length overall: 72'9"

Beam: 21 feet (6.4m)

Displacement:
Light – 71.81 long tons
Loaded – 116.07 long tons

Deck area: 230 square feet

Payload: 41.26 short tons (37.4m) or 47 combat-loaded troops

Range:
Light: 320 nautical miles
Loaded: 271 nautical miles

Draft: 4 ft. 6 in. (1.4m)

Crew size: 8 enlisted (4 per shift for 24-hour operation)

On-hand: 6

ORGANIZATION: TRANSPORTATION FLOATING CRAFT COMPANY (TOE 55889F000)

Mission. To perform floating and harbor craft operations, water terminal, water transport joint amphibious, inland waterway or logistics over the shore (JLOTS) operations.

Assignment. To a Sustainment Brigade, responsible for port and watercraft operations; normally attached to a Transportation Terminal Battalion.

Employment. The company will deploy to provide floating craft and harbor-craft support along with heavy lift services either pier or ships side. This unit is in direct support of the Transportation Terminal Battalion. The unit is modular in design and can deploy with only the personnel required to support the initial deployment and build incrementally to a full company operation.

Capabilities. At Level 1, this unit provides:
- One Large Tug for ocean and coastal towing, salvage, and recovery operations, general purpose harbor duties, and firefighting service.
- Two Small Tugs for tug services in support of water terminal and inland waterway operations.
- One Floating Crane to load and discharge heavy lift cargo that is beyond the capacity of ship's gear.
- One barge to transport up to 324 short tons of deck loaded dry cargo or 93,000 gallons of bulk fuel. Serves as a refueling point for Army watercraft operating in the area.
- Individuals of this organization can assist in the coordinated defense of the unit's area or installation. This unit performs limited field maintenance on its organic watercraft. This unit provides, to the supported unit, one cook to augment food service capability.

This unit is dependent on:
- Appropriate elements of the Transportation Terminal Battalion and Sustainment Brigade for food service, combat health support, religious, legal, finance, personnel administrative services, laundry, bath, clothing exchange services, and supplemental transportation support.
- Higher headquarters for COMSEC, communication, and automation maintenance.
- Inland Cargo Transfer Company, Seaport Operations Company, or supporting unit for automotive and generator maintenance.
- Harbormaster Detachment for coordination of watercraft operations.

• Transportation Watercraft Maintenance Company for field and sustainment maintenance.

CRAFT: 128-FOOT LARGE TUG (LT)

NSN: 1925-01-509-7013 (Modified)
LIN: T68330

Figure 2-6. 128-Foot Large Tug

Mission: The 128-foot large tug (LT) is used for ocean and coastal towing operations. It is also used to dock and undock large ships. It has a secondary mission of accomplishing general-purpose harbor duties, such as positioning floating cranes. The LT is equipped to accomplish fire-fighting duties, required where ammunition ships are being worked. It is also used to perform salvage and recovery operations for watercraft disabled or damaged along water transport LOC and to overcome anti-access and port denial activities.

Transportability: The LT is self-deployable worldwide.

Characteristics/capabilities

    Class: A2

    Length overall: 128 feet (39m)

    Beam: 36 feet (11m)

    Displacement (weight): 786 long tons (light); 1,057 long tons (loaded)

    Bollard pull: 58 long tons

    Range:
    Light: 5,000 NM at 13.5 knots
    Loaded: 5,000 NM at 12 knots

    Draft:
    Light: 14 feet
    Loaded: 16 feet

    Crew size: 23 (8 warrant officers and 15 enlisted for 24-hour operation)

    On-hand: 6

CRAFT: LARGE TUG (LT) 100-FOOT, FLIGHT III

NSN: 1925-00-375-3003

LIN: X71046

Figure 2-7. 100-Foot Large Tug, Flt III

Mission: The 100-foot large tug (LT) is used to dock and undock large oceangoing vessels and for heavy towing within harbor areas. It is also used to dock and undock large ships. Secondary functions include general utility uses, fire fighting and salvage operations. It may also conduct limited offshore towing between terminals.

Transportability: The LT is self-deployable worldwide, but usually delivered via ship or held in APS.

Characteristics/capabilities

 Class: A2

 Length overall: 107 feet (32.6m)

 Beam: 27 feet (8.2m)

 Displacement (weight): 295 long tons (light); 390 long tons (loaded)

 Bollard pull: 13.8 long tons/31.5 long tons

 Range: Light: 3,323 NM at 12.8 knots
 Loaded: 2,245 NM at 12.8 knots

 Draft: Light: 11.5 feet (3.5m)
 Loaded: 12.5 feet (3.8m2m)

 Crew size: 16 (4 warrant officers and 12 enlisted for 24-hour operation)

 On-hand: 2

CRAFT: SMALL TUG 900 (ST)

NSN: 1925-01-435-1713
LIN: T68398

Figure 2-8. Small Tug 900

Mission: The ST 900 is capable of moving cargo barges and lighterage of various types within a harbor, port, or LOTS anchorage. The ST 900 is shallow draft and of enough horsepower to tow and husband general cargo barges in harbors, inland waterways, and along coastlines, and is capable of operation in Sea State 3. It can also assist larger tugs with utility work, such as movement of ships, floating cranes, and line-handling duties.

Transportability: Deck loaded aboard LASH ships or heavy lift vessels.

Characteristics/capabilities

    Class: B

    Length overall: 60 feet (18.3m)

    Beam: 22 feet (6.7m)

    Displacement (weight): 105 long tons (light) /TBD (loaded)

    Bollard pull: 15 long tons

    Range:
    Light: 720 NM at 6 knots
    Loaded: Variable with tow
    Draft: 6 feet (1.8m)

Crew size: 12 (All enlisted; 12-hour operations. 24 hour operations when augmented by additional licensed 88K/L40 or higher)

    On-hand: 16

CRAFT: BARGE DERRICK (BD), 115-TON

NSN: 1935-01-434-6826
LIN: F36090

Figure 2-9. Barge Derrick, 115 Ton

Mission: The BD 115T is used to load and discharge heavy lift cargo that is beyond the lift or reach capacity of ship or land-based cranes. It provides the lift and reach needed to discharge the heaviest of projected Army cargo from Large Medium-Speed Roll-on/Roll-off ships (LMSR), as well as commercial container ships, to accomplish strategic deployment. It is capable of lifting a 75-ton main battle tank from the centerline of a non-self-sustaining ship. The BD 115T can be employed theater-wide anywhere water terminal or offshore operations are conducted.

Transportability: The BD 115T can be towed to overseas locations or deck loaded aboard a FLO/FLO ship for transport.

Characteristics/capabilities:

Class: A1

Length overall: 200 feet (61m)

Beam: 80 feet (24.4m)

Displacement: 1560 long tons

Boom length: 220 feet (67m)

Capacity: 115 long tons at 80-foot (24.4m) radius

Range: N/A (non-self-propelled)

Draft:
Light: 7 feet, 4 inches (2.2m)
Loaded: To be determined

Crew size: 14 (1 warrant officer and 13 enlisted for 24-hour operation)

On-hand: 4

CRAFT: BARGE, LIQUID CARGO, FUEL (BG)

NSN: 1930-00-313-9472
LIN: B31197

Figure 2-10. Barge, Liquid Cargo (Fuel)

Mission: The BG 231C is used to transport liquid or general cargo in harbors and inland waters. It can transfer liquid products from offshore tankers to shore facilities. The BG 231 can also serve as a refueling point for watercraft operating in the area. The barge is equipped with two skegs aft, thereby improving its towing capability by helping to keep it tracking on course.

Transportability: The BG 231C can be towed to overseas locations or deck loaded aboard a Heavy Lift Pre-position Ship (HLPS).

Characteristics/capabilities

> **Class:** C
>
> **Length overall:** 120 feet (36.6m)
>
> **Beam:** 33 feet (10.1m)
>
> **Displacement** (weight): 185 long tons (Light); 763 long tons (Loaded)
>
> **Cargo capacity:**
> Deck: 578 long tons
> Liquid: 4,160 barrels (188,416 gallons or 713,232 liters).
>
> **Cargo pump capacity:** 1,050 gallons per minute (3974.7 liters per minute).
>
> **Draft:**
> Light: 3 feet (0.9m)
> Loaded: 9 feet (2.7m)
>
> **Crew size:** 6 enlisted (3 per shift for 24-hour operation)
>
> **On-hand:** 4

TRANSPORTATION MODULAR CAUSEWAY COMPANY (TOE 55848F000)

Mission. To provide movement support for cargo and equipment during intra-theater lift, water terminal, water transport tactical and joint amphibious, riverine and logistics over the shore (JLOTS) operations. Modular causeway companies provide the Army with the capability to transfer cargo between ships or from ship to shore. Causeway systems provide the essential interface between Army lighterage and RO/RO ships. A modular causeway company is organized with two RRDF, one causeway ferry, and one floating causeway.

Assignment. To a Sustainment Brigade, responsible for port and watercraft operations; normally attached to a Transportation Terminal Battalion. May be attached to the U.S. Navy or U.S. Marine Corps to support joint amphibious, riverine or logistics over the shore (JLOTS) operations.

Employment. The Modular Causeway will deploy to a theater of operations to provide movement support on a 24 hour basis. The unit is modular in design and can deploy with only the personnel required to support the initial deployment and build incrementally to a full company operation.

Capabilities. This unit provides:

- One Floating Causeway (FC) pier consisting of from 1 to 17 non-powered causeway sections (CSNP) (up to 1,200 feet in length), with a dry bridge for the discharge of cargo and equipment from lighters directly to an unimproved shoreline or degraded fixed port facility.

- One Causeway Ferry (CF) consisting of one powered causeway section (CSP) and up to three non-powered causeway sections (CSNP) for moving rolling stock, break bulk, containerized cargo from ship to shore.

- Two Roll-On/Roll-Off Discharge Platforms (RRDF) consisting of up to 18 non-powered causeway sections (CSNP) each that interfaces between RO/RO ships and lighterage for the rapid discharge of rolling stock.

- Several variants of causeway section configuration to meet mission needs.

- Individuals of this organization can assist in the coordinated defense of the unit's area or installation.

- This unit performs field maintenance on all organic equipment except communication security (COMSEC) equipment.

This unit is dependent on:

- Appropriate elements of the Army Service Component Command (ASCC) for religious, legal, combat health support, finance, and personnel and administrative services.

- Seaport Operations Company, and Floating Craft Company, for assistance in assembling the causeway systems.

- Higher headquarters for communications and automation maintenance.

- Harbormaster Detachment, for lighterage control operations and the Transportation Watercraft Maintenance Company, for causeway maintenance support.

- Engineer Horizontal Construction Company, for pier maintenance and beach site survey.

- Engineer Heavy Dive Team, for pier maintenance, beach site survey.

CRAFT: MODULAR CAUSEWAY SYSTEM (RO/RO DISCHARGE FACILITY)

NSN: 1945-01-497-7059
LIN: C14572

Figure 2-11. Modular Causeway System (RO/RO Discharge Facility)

Mission: The Roll-on/Roll-off Discharge Facility (RRDF) provides the essential interface between Army lighters and RO/RO ships. It receives tracked and wheeled vehicles when driven across the RRDF from the RO/RO ship directly onto an Army lighter moored to the RRDF.

Transportability: The RRDF is constructed of modular causeway systems and can be deployed aboard container ships and other cargo vessels or via rail.

Characteristics/capabilities

Class: B

Components:
18 modular causeway sections
1 combination beach and sea-end section
2 modular/side-loadable warping tugs
1 lighting, fendering, and anchoring system

Crew size: 76 enlisted (main section: 36 enlisted; warping tug crew: 20 x 2 crews for 24-hour operation)

On-hand: 6

CRAFT: MODULAR CAUSEWAY SYSTEM (CAUSEWAY FERRY)

NSN:
LIN: Z14597

Figure 2-12. Modular Causeway System (Causeway Ferry)

Mission: The Causeway Ferry (CF) moves rolling, break-bulk, and containerized cargo from an ocean-going vessel directly to the shore-side logistics operation or to a fixed or semi-permanent pier. It will support RO/RO and LO/LO operations.

Transportability: The CF is constructed of modular causeway sections and can be deployed aboard container ships and other cargo vessels or via rail.

Characteristics/capabilities (components)
       Class: B
       Components:
     Powered modular causeway section
     2 modular causeway (intermediate) sections
1 combination beach and sea-end section

Crew size: 16 enlisted (CF: 4 enlisted; Powered section: 12 enlisted for 24-hour operation)

On-hand: 3

CRAFT: MODULAR CAUSEWAY SYSTEM (FLOATING CAUSEWAY)

NSN: 1945-01-128-7268
LIN: C14504

Figure 2-13. Modular Causeway System (Floating Causeway)

Mission: The Floating Causeway (FC) provides a dry bridge for the discharge of cargo from lighters directly to the beach. It can be emplaced in a number of configurations, with the trident configuration being the most effective for most conditions. The FC is a key LOTS enabler to overcome beach obstacles and gradients in order to permit discharge of cargo across shallow waters onto shore.

Transportability: The FC is constructed of modular causeway sections and can be deployed aboard container ships and other cargo vessels or via rail.

Characteristics/capabilities (components)
      Class: B

29.3 modular causeway (intermediate) sections
2 combination beach and sea ends
1 lighting, fendering and anchor system
2 modular/side-loadable warping tugs (powered sections)
Crew size: 38 enlisted (main segment: 18; warping tug: 10 x 2 crews for 24-hour operation)

On-hand: 3

CRAFT: MODULAR CAUSEWAY SYSTEM (WARPING TUG)

NSN: 1945-01-473-2285
LIN: W41775
Mission: The Warping Tug (WT) provides tendering functions to assemble, tow, restrain and maneuver the RRDF and FC, and to emplace and retrieve anchors.

Craft assessment: Began fielding in FY96. Completed procurement in 2008.

Transportability: The WT can be deployed aboard container ships and other cargo vessels or via rail.

Characteristics/capabilities: The modular warping tug is a self-propelled craft composed of a 40-foot section and two 20-foot raked ends which are configured into 80' x 24' sections.

Class: B

On-hand: 18

SUPPORTING ORGANIZATIONS

ORGANIZATION: TRANSPORTATION WATERCRAFT MAINTENANCE COMPANY (TOE 55613L000)

Mission. To provide field maintenance support for U.S. Army watercraft.

Assignment. To a Sustainment Brigade, responsible for port and watercraft operations; normally attached to a Transportation Terminal Battalion.

Employment. Will normally be employed to repair Army watercraft.

Capabilities. This unit provides personnel and equipment to perform field maintenance support.

- Individuals of this organization can assist in the coordinated defense of the unit's area or installation.

- This unit performs unit maintenance on all organic equipment except communications security (COMSEC) equipment.

This unit is dependent on:

- Appropriate elements of the Army Service Component Command for religious, legal, combat health support, finance, and personnel and administrative services.

- Diving support provided by the Heavy Dive Team, TOE 05530LA00, and Light Diving Team, for underwater maintenance. If required to support diving operations, the Landing Craft Utility (LCU) will be provided by the Heavy Watercraft Company, TOE 55829L000.

ORGANIZATION: TRANSPORTATION HARBORMASTER DETACHMENT (TOE 55587FA00)

Mission. To provide 24 hour operational control for Army vessels conducting intra-theater lift, water terminal, inland waterway, joint amphibious, and logistics over the shore operations.

Assignment. To a Sustainment Brigade, responsible for port and watercraft operations; normally attached to a Transportation Terminal Battalion.

Employment. This unit will operate in water ports and terminals in all areas of the world throughout the spectrum of contingency missions.

Capabilities. This unit provides:

- 24 hour operational control for Army vessel movements during intra-theater lift, water terminal, inland waterway and joint amphibious, riverine and logistics over the shore (LOTS) operations.

- Coordination for berthing and anchorage assignments for Army vessels within a terminal area controlled by the Military Sealift Command (MSC), joint, coalition, or host nation agencies.

- Short and long range vessel communications, utilizing Harbormaster Command & Control Center, to control vessel operations and monitor watercraft communications.

- Operation of the Lighterage Control Center (LCC), ship lighterage control point (SLCP) and beach lighterage control point (BLCP) in bare beach or degraded port LOTS environments. May form the nucleus for a joint lighterage control center (JLCC).

- Staff expertise for watercraft operational planning and coordination with other joint or host nation activities conducting vessel operations.

- Staff expertise for watercraft maintenance operations and planning, and coordination for vessel maintenance support with joint, host nation or contractor maintenance activities.

- Individuals of this organization can assist in the coordinated defense of the unit's area or installation.

This unit is dependent on:

- Appropriate elements of the Army Service Component Command for religious, legal, combat health support, finance, and personnel and administrative services.

- Supported company for food service and supplemental transportation and unit maintenance.

- A Combat Weather Detachment for weather forecasting support.

- Accountable maintenance support as required.

OPERATIONAL HIERARCHY

2-14. Army watercraft may be assigned to several varying command structures and levels depending on the mission and geographic location. These include but are not limited to the Theater Sustainment Command (TSC) or Expeditionary Sustainment Command (ESC). As an Army organization in support of joint maneuver operations, the Watercraft Company or detachment will most likely be assigned to the Army Service Component Command and further attached as needed to meet Combatant Commander maneuver requirements for land-based forces. Mission dependent, the watercraft may be under tactical control (TACON) or operational control (OPCON) to the JFLCC as a theater asset. Army vessels may work singularly or together with multiple detachments under the JFLCC command. This arrangement may be seen in operations with limited Army ground combat force participation such as disaster or humanitarian relief operations involving host nation personnel support.

2-15. **Command and Control (C2).** Externally, the precise C2 structure will be at the direction of the Geographical Combatant Commander (GCC), dependent on the theater and the operation. The unit's higher headquarters will establish the hierarchy for operational mission tasking. Mission orders will be directed IAW established Joint and Service C2 organizational structures, dependent on the Combatant Commander's operation. Internally, the Vessel Master - who is also the Detachment Commander in the case of large high speed vessels and logistics support vessels - commands the vessel, is responsible for all operations and duties aboard the vessel, communication with higher command and ensuring mission objectives are met. Thus, one of the most critical actions the Vessel Master will perform during deployment to a new area of employment - or during change of mission or attachment - is to clearly establish the vessel's C2 and tasking chain of command. The vessel Detachments are organized to conduct vessel-specific operations and are not designed to provide C2 for subordinate or embarked units.

2-16. When the vessel is providing operational and/or tactical maneuver to a command for maneuver support, the commander of the embarked unit is responsible for the conduct of his unit while aboard the vessel. The vessel master and the embarked unit commander will coordinate mission planning aspects as they relate to the movement of the unit and the support requirements (e.g., C4ISR support) while underway. Regardless of rank, the Vessel Master has final authority and ultimate responsibility aboard the vessel.

COMMUNICATIONS ARCHITECTURE

2-17. The vessel bridge serves as the command post (CP) in both peacetime and wartime environments. The Vessel Master is responsible for all external and internal vessel communications, which are configured so they can be conducted from the bridge if required. The CP remains operational whether static or underway. On the Bridge, an Electronic Chart Display Information System (ECDIS) or similar system will be used to provide an accurate common operating picture of navigation and vessel traffic. The ECDIS will be capable of displaying electronic charts for the local area and tracking the course that the ship makes along this chart. On certain vessels, an Integrated Bridge System (IBS) is installed that facilitates detailed waypoint navigation, alarms, and radar target inputs integrated into a single monitor. All of this information, displayed on one screen, allows the navigator to immediately understand the status of the vessel in relation to the surrounding environment. When IBS is integrated, it provides the vessel with a significant safety enhancement over traditional ECDIS. A land-based Harbormaster Detachment provides the link to the vessel for land-based units.

2-18. Whether using fixed ports, undeveloped or degraded ports or JLOTS sites, the Harbormaster Command and Control Center's C4ISR capability provides continuous vessel tracking, and communications among the services, coalition, commercial and host nation vessels and elements. Constant vessel tracking is critical to successful, safe operations. Further, the Harbormaster Detachment must maintain constant interoperability with the supported command of which it is a part via the Army-operated LandWarNet, as well as the Maritime Force via the Navy-operated FORCENet, and Coalition, multi-national, and/or inter-agency organizations as appropriate to the mission. The Harbormaster Command and Control Center (HCCC) enables the unit to conduct split-based operations with main and remote operations capabilities. All of the vessel's C4ISR architecture and capability is designed to allow the vessel and the embarked force to become an integral element of the Common Operating Picture (COP). Through a tracking system (such as the Movements Tracking System, MTS), mobile sensors provide critical input to the COP of platforms on the battlefield, while the vessel and its embarked forces leverage the COP to conduct Joint expeditionary operations. The Vessel COP capabilities can include the following:

- Current locations and all available status information for friendly, neutral, and enemy ground, maritime, and air units.

- All available planned movement information for friendly, neutral, and enemy ground, maritime, and air units.

- All available information that could impact the disposition of friendly, neutral, and enemy ground, maritime, and air units (e.g., weather, Battle Damage Assessment (BDA)).

- Generated features and projections (e.g., battle plans, operating zones, fly-through depictions).

CONCEPT OF SUPPORT

2-19. **Integrated Logistics Support.** As is normal with any major items of equipment in the services' inventories, the vessels operated by the Army are supported by established Army support systems and infrastructure. While many vessels are resourced by the Army, they all operate as part of a global maritime fleet that supports the full range of joint operations and services. Thus, they are supported by an integrated logistics system that leverages Navy and Army, as well as commercial, support capabilities.

2-20. **Logistics Support.** Vessel-specific support such as berthing, fresh water, provisioning, shore power, fuel, and waste management services are provided by the vessel's assigned chain-of-command while the unit is at its home station and prior to deployment. In most cases, the larger vessels will not require en route logistical support, as they can access both Army and Naval support channels while en route when needed. The vessels are also capable of accessing contractor and locally-provided commercial support services and facilities. Once they arrive in the Joint Operating Area (JOA), and during operations in a remote theater of operation, vessels will obtain logistics services through the joint logistics command or system in place in that theater.

2-21. **Maintenance.** Due to the expeditionary nature of the operations that Army watercraft are called on to perform, they are capable of sustained operations with little or no available external maintenance support structure when deployed for short periods. Most Army vessels are designed with redundant systems to allow continued operations when certain systems fail through normal use. Upgrades and modernization strategies occur on a system-by-system basis. Soldiers are trained to perform field and limited sustainment maintenance on organic equipment and internal systems related to vessel operations. While the crew can perform emergency troubleshooting on communications equipment, the vessel is not resourced to maintain communication security (COMSEC) equipment and systems. The vessel crew is capable of leveraging local contractor and host-nation maintenance facilities and shipyards, and will coordinate with the Harbormaster Detachment and the Army's Watercraft Field Maintenance Company for reinforcing field and sustainment maintenance support when required.

2-22. **Unit Support.** While watercraft units are organized to conduct sustained stand-alone operations, they are not designed to operate independently of normal C2 support channels. While operating at home station the vessels crews will be supported by their higher C2 element. All medical, finance, personnel and administrative services, personnel billeting, level II and III health care, unit sustainment training and deployment readiness requirements will be supported by the home station chain-of-command. Once deployed into the JOA, those functions will be provided by the chain-of-command to which the unit is attached or assigned. Class A1 and A2 vessels are capable of providing unit-level health service and food service support as described in Chapter 2.

MARITIME TRAINING

2-23. The strategy for training Army Mariners is built on an integrated approach that includes institutional and unit training, as well as continuing professional development and certifications in accordance with AR 56-9 Watercraft. Modern and updated training is vital for successful water transport operations and only grows in importance as the Army strives toward a global maneuver capability. Modernizing the way in which Army mariners receive training is required as we modernize the fleet. The use of virtual and distance learning takes advantage of advances in technology. Increased use of full-feature simulations for both deck and engineers is a must.

SIMULATIONS

2-24. Given the cost of vessel operations and the feasibility of real-world training at distant ports and operating sites, a key element of the Army Watercraft training strategy will continue to be the extensive use of simulations. Currently, the Army operates two vessel simulation facilities - one on the East Coast at Fort Eustis, Virginia and one on the West Coast at Mare Island, California. These facilities provide a wide range of simulations, to include integrated bridge operation for all Army vessels, inclement weather and damage control operations, and the ability to simulate a number of ports around the world. The facility at Fort Eustis includes an engine room simulator that provides underway engine operations and trouble-shooting training. Potential development in simulation include:

- Increased simulation training as a viable alternative to develop and maintain diverse operational skills.

- Increased Force Protection training for operators and leaders, to include development of vessel force protection simulator and simulations should be considered as part of the tactical port operations capability development.

- Development and implementation of system specific training for low density military occupation skill (MOS) personnel within the watercraft field.

JOINT TRAINING

2-25. The idea that the Future Force needs to be able to operate from the littorals is widely acknowledged. Thus, in accordance with Future Force concepts, the Army is currently exploring how to leverage emerging capabilities and concepts. Although the Army will likely continue to employ land bases as the primary means of force projection, future Joint concepts dictate that our Leaders be trained in deployment from the sea. The Transportation Corps is pursuing a program to develop and integrate appropriate modeling and simulation training into its Leader development programs. Our training strategy will include integration of this effort with Naval modeling, simulation, and training initiatives in order to increase Inter-Service understanding and interoperability, while also advancing Watercraft Leaders' skills.

2-26. The Joint Training Information Management System (JTIMS) is a web-based system providing automated support to the Joint Training System (JTS). The system is used by the joint staff and major commands to manage all large-scale, military training and operational events. The JTS provides a multi-phase methodology for aligning training strategy with assigned missions while optimizing application of scarce resources. JTIMS supports the task-based, closed-loop features of the JTS by facilitating the development of an integrated, task-based thread to guide all four JTS phases. Training requirements, plans, events, and assessments are all linked to mission and mission essential tasks. Entry of supporting planning data into JTIMS is required during planning of joint exercises such as Joint Logistics over the Shore (JLOTS) exercises using Afloat Prepositioned Stock (APS) equipment.

TRANSPORTATION SCHOOL MARITIME TRAINING

2-27. The U. S. Army Transportation School fields a trained and ready force of Army mariners. Training the force begins with Training and Doctrine Command (TRADOC) and carries over to the Active and Reserve component units. The high level of skill an Army mariner is expected to attain and maintain requires that frequent crew and unit training be performed at sea. While strong training programs emphasize hands-on underway operations, Training Aids, Devices, Simulators and Simulations (TADSS) complement underway training and are integral to providing a trained and ready force. Vessel Bridge and Engine Room simulators and simulations familiarize and stress vessel crews in performing intricate underway maneuvers during heavy sea conditions, limited visibility and in less than ideal conditions are critical to ensuring that mariners can perform watercraft operations worldwide.

HIGH SPEED VESSEL TRAINING

2-28. The high speed vessels are unique in Army watercraft in that it is designed to operationally move unit sets. The JHSV in construction is the first Army watercraft designed to move personnel and equipment together in a ready-to-fight configuration. This will require new approaches to training, requiring each course to emphasize the unique nature of this craft as an operational platform as opposed to simply a logistics vessel.

2-29. HSV training includes onboard computer training without increasing the training burden on the institution or operator or placing undue reliability burdens on the control systems and indicators at the individual platform level. This embedded training is used before, during, and after deployment, allowing crews to digitally train in the environment in which they will fight, and to conduct en route mission planning and rehearsals. Proper operation must be simple enough so that frequent, extensive retraining is not required to maintain operator and maintainer proficiency.

2-30. Appropriate training aids, devices, simulators, and simulations (TADSS) must be available for the institutional training base as well as HSV-equipped units. HSV systems and subsystems must be designed to conduct training to facilitate individual, crew, and organizational training proficiency. Embedded simulations will also permit mission planning and rehearsal in both stand-alone and computer-based modes. JHSV employs simulations training, combining for both unit training and operational missions.

2-31. Training for the HSV consists of four courses:

- High Speed Craft Safety Course (HSCS) – Distributed Learning.

- High Speed Craft Deck Systems (HSCDS) – Institutional.

- High Speed Craft Engineering Systems (HSCES) – Institutional.

- High Speed Craft Brigade Resource Management (BRM) –Institutional.

2-32. Maintaining skilled and highly capable crews for Army watercraft requires a total commitment to training. This commitment must include ensuring resources for the training aids and simulators necessary for use by instructors in the Transportation School are available to allow operators/maintainers to practice their skills in an operational environment. Continued review of POIs, development of improved training methods, use of new technology and continued execution of JLOTS exercises, and other unit training missions will ensure a trained, proficient staff of Army mariners now and in the future.

2-33. Army watercraft requires specially-trained Soldiers who are capable of performing soldier tasks, as well as conduct maritime operations. Extensive simulator training is the norm on all Army watercraft navigation and engineer troubleshooting systems.   Upon completion of entry level training in marine navigation and maintenance/engineering methods, Army mariners are provided advanced training that includes traditional classroom settings, simulators, and hands-on experience. Fully integrated, non-detachable, embedded training capability are incorporated into the vessels to the greatest extent possible to support and maintain individual, section and crew collective training at home station or while underway. The Army mariners assigned to the HSV require training specialized for high-speed vessel operations and navigation, and require training on the transformational maintenance engineering systems aboard the craft.

2-34. The Army trains its maritime personnel in accordance with AR 56-9, which closely mirrors the requirements of the International Maritime Organization (IMO), Standards of Training, Certification, and Watch keeping (STCW) and applicable United States Code of Federal Regulations.   Army training is continuously updated and modernized as it follows the commercial maritime industry training standards. Individual and crew training focuses on inclusion of maritime technology, operations, and maintenance techniques as they are employed in the Joint operational environment. Operating at high speed requires additional training in accordance with the International Code of Safety for High Speed Craft, as it travels at considerably faster speeds and may have a different hull design, operating parameters, and propulsion system than other Army watercraft.

PERSONNEL: SOLDIER-MARINERS

2-35. Following are definitions for the positions aboard Army Water Transport systems, including watercraft, causeway, cranes, etc.

Master. The master is in command of the vessel. As such, the master is responsible for ensuring the vessel is operated efficiently, safely, and economically by strictly complying with Army regulations, federal and environmental laws. Other duties include enforcing safety, and maintaining vessel logs and records.

Chief Engineer. The chief engineer is responsible to the master for the efficient, safe, and economical operation of the engine department. Duties include maintaining vessel maintenance logs, records, reports and inventory of repair parts. Additionally, the chief engineer directs & supervises maintenance and repair of vessel equipment in accordance with AR 750-1 and Maintenance Allocation Chart (MAC).

Chief Mate. The chief mate serves as assistant to the master The chief mate is responsible for all deck operations and maintenance of deck department equipment. When required, the chief mate also navigates the vessel during appropriate watches.

First Assistant Engineer. As assistant to the chief engineer, the first assistant engineer supervises the engine department, to include engine personnel training, safety, maintenance and general ship's business. Additionally, he stands underway watch as Engineering-Officer-of-the-Watch (EOOW).

Mate. The mate assists the master by navigating the vessel during appropriate watches. The mate supervises the navigation department to include plotting course, maintaining bridge equipment, and maintaining sea pay records. Other duties include supervision of galley operations and personnel to include ordering subsistence, acquiring subsistence funds to support the mission, and insuring proper health and welfare. The mate also performs duties as medical officer.

Assistant Engineer. The assistant engineer assists the Chief and 1st Asst Engineer by supervising maintenance on auxiliaries, D.C., A/C, emergency generators, bow thruster, rescue boat, and hydraulic equipment. Stands underway watch as EOOW. Also functions as property book, supply and voyage funds officer. As such, he or she is responsible for all vessel supply functions, inventories and maintenance sustainment tracking to include supervising the ordering and tracking of all classes of material order for vessels consumption.

Detachment Sergeant. The detachment sergeant is responsible to the Master for the training, safety, and good conduct of the Detachment enlisted personnel. When required, the detachment sergeant maintains qualifications for underway watch and stands watch.

Marine Operations NCO. As the Non-Commissioned Officer In Charge (NCOIC), the marine operations NCO is responsible for all aspects of Modular Causeway System operations.

Marine Maintenance NCO. The marine maintenance NCO is the section sergeant for the engineering department and stands underway watch as Engineer NCOIC of the Watch when required.

Boatswain. The boatswain is responsible for maintenance and reporting operational conditions of the deck department machinery and equipment. In additions, the boatswain is responsible for the conduct, discipline, and direct supervision of deck personnel. The boatswain also supervises preparation of the vessel for sea, and cargo or towing operations and stands underway watch as appropriate.

Junior Marine Engineer. The junior marine engineer assists the assistant engineer as directed and stands underway watch as Engineer NCOIC of the Watch.

Food Service Sergeant. The food service sergeant operates the ship's galley and is responsible for maintenance of food preparation equipment and area, food preparation, ensuring food handlers' personal hygiene, preparing requests for rations, coordinating ration delivery, and menu preparation. The first cook also prepares and serves meals. This position requires familiarization with emergency station bill and participation in all vessel drills and emergencies.

Leading Seaman. The lead seaman assists the mate and boatswain in planning and preparing for vessel operations. Duties include maintaining all navigation equipment and publications. Additionally, the lead seaman stands underway watch as appropriate and assists the Boatswain by supervising deck operations and maintenance as required.

Senior Marine Engineman. The senior marine engineman assists the Assistant Engineer as directed and stands underway watch as Engineer NCOIC of the Watch.

Emergency Care Sergeant. The emergency care sergeant is responsible to the master for recording all medical emergencies and provision of emergency medical care of all crew and passengers. Duties include providing emergency treatment for injuries, cardiopulmonary resuscitation, ensures surgical instruments and medical supplies are maintained onboard. The emergency care sergeant is required to be familiar with procedures for birth and death at sea, prevention and control of shipboard and communicable diseases, and telemedicine procedures. This position requires familiarization with emergency station bill and participation in all vessel drills and emergencies.

Senior Radio Operator/Maintainer. The senior radio operator/maintainer is responsible for operating and maintaining the vessel's communications equipment. He also stands underway watch as radio operator. This position requires familiarization with emergency station bill and participation in all vessel drills and emergencies.

Radio Operator/Maintainer. The radio operator/maintainer assists in operating and maintaining the vessel's communications equipment and stands underway watch as Radio Operator. This position requires familiarization with emergency station bill and participation in all vessel drills and emergencies.

Seaman. The seaman assists the Boatswain in maintaining and operating all equipment and in the conduct of cargo on load and deck offload operations. Other duties include standing underway watch as helmsman and lookout when required.

Marine Engineman. The marine engineman assists in maintaining/operating vessel's main propulsion systems, generators and electrical systems. Other duties include standing underway watch assisting the Engineer NCO of the Watch as required.

Coxswain. The coxswain is the master on Class B Vessels and responsible for all aspects of vessel operations.

Crane Operator. The crane operator operates the barge crane in support of lift operations, as directed. This position requires familiarization with emergency station bill and participation in all vessel drills and emergencies.

Senior Forklift Operator. The senior forklift operator is responsible for operating and maintaining various types of forklifts in support of Modular Causeway System (MCS) operations. This position requires familiarization with emergency station bill and participation in all vessel drills and emergencies.

Petroleum Specialist. The petroleum specialist conducts watercraft fueling operations in accordance with regulation. This position requires familiarization with emergency station bill and participation in all vessel drills and emergencies.

RT Forklift Operator. The RT forklift operator assists in operating and maintaining Rough Terrain forklifts in support of MCS operations. This position requires familiarization with emergency station bill and participation in all vessel drills and emergencies.

Cook. The cook prepares and serves two to three meals daily while underway, as directed. This position requires familiarization with emergency station bill and participation in all vessel drills and emergencies.

SUMMARY

2-36. Army Watercraft provides a wide variety of capabilities to support land combat power deployment distribution and sustainment throughout the maritime domain. The crew is trained to be inherently multi-functional, providing a wide spectrum of on-board capabilities to support practically any mission required. The combination of multi-capable military vessels and multi-functional military crews provides an organic Army maneuverable and sustainable capability for maneuver and along coastal areas, into littorals and inland waterways that compliments organic air and land maneuver capabilities.

This page intentionally left blank.

Chapter 3

Projecting the Land Force

Due to the increase of worldwide asymmetric threats to our National interests, the U.S. military is working to adapt to these threats and confront the enemy whenever and wherever need be. This requirement drives the need for speed and the ability to move not only equipment, but also combat ready soldiers of the land force in tactical environments forward of the strategic port. Army watercraft exists almost wholly to support the ground force commander.

THE OPERATIONAL ENVIRONMENT

3-1.   Anti-access and access denial (AA/AD) strategies developed by our adversaries have greatly diminished the option to extend global influence through forward basing of military capabilities. This problem is substantiated in the 2008 Joint Operating Environment (JOE) Study. The solution that supports the National Military Strategy while countering AA/AS challenges is the development of a new for projection paradigm: "Deploy = Employ". The "Deploy = Employ Paradigm" as defined in TRADOC PAM 525-3-6, Para 4-e(3) states, "The fielding of advanced air and sea lift platforms will enable prompt responding Army formations to deploy in combat ready unit configurations, with integrated sustainment, in a matter of days, with units prepared to begin operations immediately after arrival." TRADOC PAM 525-3-6 further states, "Joint austere access, high speed sealift (AAHSS), theater watercraft such as the joint high speed vessel (JHSV), super short take off and landing (SSTOL), and heavy lift vertical take-off and landing (HLVTOL) aircraft, and advanced joint logistics over the shore (JLOTS) will permit the JF and ground force commander to push substantial, ready to fight land power ashore through multiple, unimproved entry points." It has been identified that the "Future Force lacks the capability to strategically deploy and immediately employ forces of battalion size or greater through austere sea-air ports of debarkation in order to support the deploy=employ paradigm, as described in the Move concept, and defeat enemy anti-access strategies. Army watercraft provides the ability to rapidly project credible, integrated, joint combat power and sustainment. This includes defeating anti-access challenges while setting the conditions for the rapid build-up of combat power through the use of simultaneous force flows by air and sea via multiple and if necessary, austere entry points.

THREAT ENVIRONMENT

3-2.   The current and projected global environment requires U.S. forces to operate in potentially hostile regions. With limited and unpredictable overseas access, basing and over-flight rights, our leadership must increasingly rely on expeditionary forces for quick response to developing crises. This places an emphasis on gaining access to contested areas as well as providing persistent presence. Littoral regions contain over three-quarters of the world's population, over eighty percent of the world's capital cities, and nearly all of the marketplaces for international trade. Because of the increasingly joint character of warfare, critical, interdependent littoral operations will take place simultaneously in the air, in space, on the ground and at sea. These facts mean the littorals are no longer a distinctly maritime domain - the littorals are increasingly a critical area of the operational environment that involves a complex intersection of three of the Joint Force Operations domains: sea, land and air. Denial of one domain by enemy or natural forces requires military access to the others.

3-3.   Potential adversaries possess an inventory of increasingly sophisticated and overlapping sensors, command and control systems, platforms, and weapons designed to deny access to littoral areas. Many of these systems are specifically built to deny the U.S. the ability to project its military instrument of National power. Enemy capabilities for area denial will vary significantly and our ability to overcome them will depend on doctrine, strategy, speed of deployment, equipment in use and its maintenance, and the level of training of military forces. Army watercraft provides a significant capability set to overcome area denial.

3-4.   Threats to the Army watercraft include air, surface, and subsurface threats in conventional as well as nuclear, biological and chemical warfare. Threat platforms may employ a mix of weaponry to include guns, shoulder fired weapons, anti-ship cruise missiles (ASCM), torpedoes, bombs, mines, improvised explosive devices, and unmanned Undersea Vehicles (UUVs). While Army watercraft do not provide combat power from the sea as the Navy does, they operate as a fully capable combat force in the uncertain threat environment described in the Joint Operational Environment. The combatant commander ensures protection for assets operating within the air, land and sea domains within the operational area, including over the horizon, inclusive of operations. The Army capability set includes: the JHSV, to leverage its operational speed, interoperability with intelligence support, situational awareness and force protection capabilities of land- and sea-based combatant assets as key elements of its force protection capabilities; Lighters such as LSV, LCU and LCM to complement this capability with heavy lift access into austere ports and onto bare beaches; Tugs and cranes to provide access into austere ports requiring salvage and port clearance; and Causeway systems to link that last 50 yards over shallow gradient beaches. All Army watercraft will face a range of challenging weather and climatic conditions and environments in their areas of operation.

VESSEL EMPLOYMENT ACROSS FULL SPECTRUM OPERATIONS

3-5.   Army Watercraft fills a critical capability gap in the ability of the Army to conduct operational maneuver in support of the Joint Force. As such, they provide critical capabilities needed to ensure ground combat forces are successful across the full spectrum operations. Thus, the first step in understanding how the fleet will be employed by land maneuver commanders is to understand the capability link to full spectrum operations.

3-6.   When employed across full spectrum operations, watercraft provides the land maneuver commander with overarching capability sets required to meet the demands of the operational environment. Those capability sets are Global Response, Force Closure, Movement and Maneuver, and Distributed Support and Sustainment.

GEOGRAPHIC RESPONSE

3-7.   The nation's capability to provide rapid, credible, global military response options to the President and to our geographic combatant commanders (GCC) has never been more important than it is in our current strategic environment. In 2003 the Army repositioned and restructured the Army watercraft fleet and associated force structure to meet the demands of our strategic environment. These actions were a direct result of the Army Watercraft Master Plan and Total Army Analysis 2009. The goal of those directives was to position the existing and future watercraft fleet to better support the GCC. The changes improve the ability of the fleet to respond to GCC requirements.

3-8.   The plan described in the following paragraphs balances requirements with the need to support our CONUS training base and COCOM Global operational requirements. Vessel allocation and stationing strategy are focused on supporting national security and defense strategies. The plan is grounded on a mix of vessels that are forward-stationed and pre-positioned in tailored packages to meet training and regional support requirements. CONUS-based vessels are maintained at the minimum essential levels to meet unit and individual training requirements for CONUS units and to meet operational requirements in the Western Hemisphere. Each of the packages can support operations in another theater as required. The following paragraphs describe the concept of employment of these support packages.

CONUS WATERCRAFT MISSION SETS

3-9.   The CONUS package is dedicated to supporting Southern Command (SOUTHCOM), Northern Command (NORTHCOM), CONUS-based missions and providing reinforcement for major combat operations worldwide as required. Additionally, the CONUS-based package supports CONUS-based unit training and exercises and provides current institutional training support to the U.S. Army Transportation School. OCONUS and Prepositioned Watercraft Mission Sets.

3-10. The two primary OCONUS support packages are tailored to provide theater-specific intra-theater lift of forces forward of the strategic port; sustainment, port opening, recovery, salvage activities, port denial/anti-access, and LOTS operations Forward stationing and pre-positioning Army watercraft in theater significantly reduces the response time to support combatant commanders' timelines, and represents a tremendous improvement in increased payload capability available to the combatant command. Pre-positioned vessels are stored and maintained in theater by the Army Materiel Command (AMC) at a reduced operational status. Reduced operational status requires vessels are fully mission-capable within a pre-determined amount of time of crews being deployed to activate the pre-positioned assets. The manning concept for pre-positioned craft requires CONUS-based crews to deploy the pre-positioned vessels and restore the craft to full mission capability within combatant command–approved timelines.

3-11. All vessels allocated to the OCONUS support packages are pre-positioned without crews. By maintaining tailored packages of pre-positioned vessels in theater, crews can be deployed within hours to begin operations shortly after arrival in the AOR. This avoids lengthy vessel transit times from CONUS bases or aboard strategic sealift, and increases response times dramatically.

3-12. The OCONUS stationing plan accounts for combatant commander requirements. As the JHSV is fielded and its overall effect on intra-theater sealift requirements will be validated, and synergy with prepositioned assets evaluated.

3-13. The medium boat detachment provides the capability for riverine and inland waterway operations, port security augmentation, and amphibious assault augmentation. The maintenance craft provides support for contact maintenance and repair of vessels operating within the AOR.

3-14. Large tugs (LT 800) are provided for vessel recovery and open-ocean towing requirements. Tugs provide the recovery capability for vessels requiring emergency tow, serves as the prime mover for the barge derrick crane during open-ocean towing, and positions the barges for lift and refueling operations. The tug also provides the capability to tow commercial barges that may be required to support mission requirements. When LT800 are not available, the FLT III Large Tug may be used "in lieu of".

3-15. Small tugs (ST 900) are provided in each support package for port management; docking and undocking assistance to smaller vessels; and for inland waterway operations. These tugs also provide significant capabilities during LOTS operations when using causeways.

3-16. Each forward support package includes two types of barges: the barge derrick (BD) 115-ton floating crane for heavy lift support and degraded port recovery and salvage operations, and the fuel barge to support the package with marine-grade fuel.

3-17. The final portion of the pre-positioned support packages is a causeway company. Each company provides roll-on/roll-off discharge facilities; causeway ferry (CF), including warping tugs; and floating causeway to provide in-stream discharge and bare-beach JLOTS capability.

Request for Forces (Watercraft)

3-18. Even with forward stationing and prepositioning of vessels and crew, a combatant commander may have increased requirements for maneuver of forces across maritime intra-theater, littorals, or inland waterways. When this occurs, the CCDR may submit a Request for Forces (RFF) through appropriate channels.

3-19. Joint High Speed Vessels will be operated by the Army with a military crew and by the Navy with a Military Sealift Command crew. Although the vessels have the same hull form, there are inherent mission sets for each service including Geneva Convention implication for MSC civilian manned vessels. The Army JHSV will provide direct support to the ground force commander, while the Navy JHSV will provide a general support platform, similar to a maritime "truck". Mutual service efficiencies such as training and maintenance are under analysis.

ARMY PRE-POSITIONED STOCKS (APS) - WATERCRAFT

3-20. Under the Army's APS concept all personnel and a minimum amount of unit equipment deploy from home station via strategic airlift. Equipment that typically deploys with unit personnel includes to-accompany-troops (TAT) materiel, such as individual weapons and chemical detection equipment (CDE), and not-authorized prepositioning (NAP) materiel. NAP is authorized unit materiel, such as some munitions and selected communications items that, for various reasons (cost, availability, sensitivity, and unsuitability for storage), are not authorized for storage at APS sites and must be brought from home station or elsewhere to complete the unit set. Chapter 6 in AR 710-1, Management of Army Prepositioned Stocks, provides direction, guidance and outlines responsibilities for prepositioned items.

3-21. Commanders of watercraft units, and leaders who may be directed to draw prepositioned watercraft, must be intimately familiar with what is and is not included in the prepositioned unit sets. Units deploying to prepositioned equipment must refer to FM 3-35.1 Prepositioned Operations for unit roles and responsibilities leading up to and including deployment. AMC is the executive agent for prepositioned stocks and is responsible for creating and updating the Automated Battlebook System (ABS). From the ABS, deploying units can create the deployment equipment list (DEL) to compare with their property book to determine the additional equipment that they must bring from home station. The deploying unit will not send anything needed for immediate use upon arrival from home station via sealift, as this would incur delays and negate the advantages of employing APS equipment. Unit equipment not mission essential early in an operation may be sent by strategic lift for subsequent link-up with the deployed force, however, commanders must be cognizant of the long delays associated with shipping equipment via sealift.

3-22. Watercraft unit commanders must have an up to date copy and be totally familiar with the individual battlebooks for the prepositioned watercraft equipment sets in each theater of operations. ABS documents can be accessed directly from the Army Knowledge Online (AKO) website at https://battleweb.army mil. Select "Site Map", "Army Organizations", "Logistics" then the TPE/ABS Battleweb link. Once on the ABS Battleweb site, choose the area and function required. When reviewing proposed changes to requirement and authorization documents (TOEs & MTOEs), care must be taken to ensure that these changes do not adversely affect the status of prepositioned systems and the unit's ability to rapidly deploy and activate the prepositioned assets. Of particular importance, leaders at senior staff level who impact TOEs and equipment lists must make sure that what is coded as TAT/NAP equipment is logical and viable in order to meet the intent of the Army Prepositioning policies and guidance.

3-23. Prepositioned watercraft are equipped and configured in accordance with applicable authorization documents and regulations. They do not include unauthorized modifications that the unit and/or crew may have installed. Units will not include these unauthorized items in TAT equipment being shipped to the prepositioning site.

3-24. Higher echelon commanders and staffs with subordinate watercraft organizations must be aware of the impacts of activating prepositioned watercraft. Because of the low density of Army watercraft systems, activation of prepositioned watercraft immediately impacts the readiness of CONUS based watercraft systems and organizations. In most cases the CONUS based vessels will be left without a crew, impacting the unit's ability to maintain the stay behind equipment. When deciding which units will activate prepositioned vessels, consideration must be given the status of the vessels in storage as well as the type unit activating the vessels. For example, if an LSV detachment is to activate a number of prepositioned LCUs, commanders and staffs must recognize the TAT equipment requirements to physically activate the craft. Although the personnel requirements can be met, the equipment requirements may not.

3-25. Activation of prepositioned Army watercraft is different than activating ground equipment. More planning and coordination is required due to the very nature of the assets being activated. By requiring the unit to bring too much equipment or by allowing the unit to bring too much "just in case" gear, the commander responsible to activate prepositioned watercraft may jeopardize their ability to accomplish the mission.

3-26. Below is an overview and guidance for the release and use of Army Pre-positioned Watercraft.

Conditions under which APS may be released are:

- Major Combat Operations (MCO). APS will be released as directed by the Chairman, Joint Chiefs of Staff, or the Chief of Staff, Army, to support an MCO. In the event of an imminent attack or capture by hostile forces, the senior Army commander present has the authority to order the immediate release of APS. As soon as the situation permits, the action taken will be reported through command channels to DCS, G-4 (ATTN: DALO-FPP).

- Small-Scale Contingencies (SSC)/National Emergencies. APS will be released by DCS, G-3/5/7, in support of SSC/national emergencies.

- Peacetime emergencies. APS will be released by DCS, G-4, in conjunction with DCS, G-3/5/7 in support of peacetime emergencies.

- Exercise support. MACOMs may request APS to validate war reserve materiel "draw" procedures during an approved AMC/MACOM exercise. The requesting MACOM will forward justification to HQDA (DALO-FPP) requesting use of stocks.

Procedures for release of APS:

- MCO. HQDA will direct the release execution.

- SSC/National Emergencies/Peacetime emergencies/Exercises. Requests for release will proceed from the requesting ACOM to DCS, G-4 (ATTN: DALO-FPP). DALO-FPP will staff the request with all responsible HQDA staff elements for evaluation and formulation of the DA position. Once the position is approved/disapproved by the ARSTAF, DALO-FPP will notify the requester. If approval is granted to use APS assets, DALO-FPP will provide written authorization to AMC/USAMMA to direct release of the stock by loan or issue.

3-27. HQDA must approve all issues and loans of APS stock to meet emergency peacetime requirements with the following exception: the AMC/USAMMA Inventory Materiel Management Centers (IMMC) may authorize issue of secondary items (spares, repair parts, and Class VIII consumables) to fill emergency peacetime operational requirements (issue priority designation (IPD) 01-03, not mission capable (NMC) requisitions only).

- IMMC managers will maintain an audit trail until APS assets are reconstituted.

- The AMC/USAMMA IMMCs will inform DCS, G-4 if problems with replenishment actions are encountered.

Note: Receiving unit will be charged for secondary items.

3-28. Control of items approved for loan will be transferred to the responsible/accountable officer(s) designated by the MACOM commander. At a minimum, the MACOM will:

- Ensure APS equipment loaned to a subordinate unit/task force or element will not be further loaned or transferred from the initial recipient without written approval of HQDA, unless outlined in the initial request from the MACOM.

- Check property accountability procedures, in accordance with AR 710-2 and AR 735-5, and will be established and maintained throughout the period of the loan. Accountable or property book officers will be appointed for units/ task forces or elements that would not otherwise deploy with an individual responsible for maintaining property accountability. Additional requirements are outlined in AR 725-50, Requisition, Receipt, and Issue System, chapter 9, and AR 710-3, Asset and Transaction Reporting System.

- Make sure TM 10/20 technical standards will be strictly enforced at time of issue and turn-in of all loaned or issued APS equipment in accordance with AR 750-1, unless previously agreed upon in writing by all parties (DCS, G-3/5/7 and G-4, AMC/OTSG, and requesting MACOMs). The MACOM will reimburse the APS releaser (AMC/USAMMA) for any direct repair, technical inspection labor, packing, crating, transportation, preservation, protection costs, and cost to return to 10/20 standards and storage incurred as a result of the loan or issue of equipment.

- Ensure equipment loaned in support of an operation will be returned to APS.

3-29. MACOM/Unit responsibility for loaned equipment:

- The borrowing MACOM will ensure that subordinate commanders who assume direct and supervisory responsibility for the equipment do not substitute like or similar items. Equipment identified by serial number or data plate information will be the same equipment returned to the issuing activity as verified by serial number/data plate identification.

- Guidance for the loan of Army equipment is contained in AR 700-131, AR 710-2, and AR 725-50. An example request and approval letter may be found in Appendix C of this FM.

SUMMARY

3-30. The essence of Army Water transport operations capability supports operational maneuver, sustains the operating forces once employed, re-deploys or re-employs combat power upon mission completion, all forward of the strategic port and encompassed in tactical operations. From a logistician's perspective, Army water transport capability is a key piece in the distribution of forces and sustainment in military and non-military operations. More importantly, from a combat arms perspective, Army water transport capability enables maneuver and facilitates sustainment missions. The Joint High Speed Vessel (JHSV), and the innovative application of current Army watercraft platforms, blends the functions of Deploy, Employ and Sustain.

3-31. Army watercraft are an integral part of the commander's scheme of maneuver. Changes to how we employ our current fleet, and develop and field future platforms are extensions of Army platform maneuverability. Transformation of the Army watercraft fleet is underway to ensure missions are met, today and tomorrow.

Chapter 4

Planning Water Transport Operations

Army/Joint planners within the theater must plan for the deployment of vessels and crew, movement of cargo, opening of new ports, unimproved facilities and beaches to accommodate throughput of cargo via areas made untenable by enemy actions. Plans should include the means of deployment (transshipment port-to-port or LOTS), proposed location and layout of the area, type of lighterage to be used, the task organization needed to attain the desired tonnage capacity, and other planning factors listed in this and subsequent chapters. Plans must also include U.S. and host nation or allied Coast Guard port security capability. Furthermore, planners must consider and should incorporate available host nation and allied capability as appropriate for watercraft operations in all conditions.

Sites should be selected based primarily on the existing capability to accommodate the desired tonnage and to facilitate operational maneuver. Major factors to consider when selecting discharge sites include threat assessment for the area, tide and tidal range, surf, pier height, beach gradients, sand bars, characteristics of the bottom and beach surface, anchorage areas, weather, throughput capability, and topographic features. See Chapter 5 for additional details in selection of beaches for LOTS.

Using water transport units over widely dispersed locations along a coastline or inland waterway requires careful evaluation of the maintenance system supporting these operations. When operationally dispersed, increased organizational maintenance must be emphasized. Unit maintenance personnel should be well trained. Every effort must be made to fix minor troubles to prevent costly equipment breakdowns. Standing operating procedures (SOP) should establish the method for providing maintenance support during operations. Floating craft maintenance units supporting Army water transport units over an extended length of coastline require mobile marine repair facilities and on-site repair service that may include the Containerized Maintenance Facility (CMF) or Forward Repair System (FRS).

Dispersing water transport units greatly increases reliance on radio communications for effective command, control, and coordination. Therefore, communications security (COMSEC) and electronic communications countermeasures (ECCM) are even more critical to maintaining reliable communications. Signal support must be planned and coordinated in advance for all watercraft missions, especially for missions requiring satellite support.

OPERATIONAL PLANNING

4-1.   Watercraft in operations must be well-planned to achieve a balanced operation. The turnaround time of the lighters must match (as closely as possible) the unloading and loading cycle of the port operating units involved. Balance cannot be maintained unless craft are unloaded at discharge points at least as fast as they are loaded at shipside or shore terminal. Every effort must be made to ensure that enough lighters are available to accept and deliver all the cargo that the port operating personnel can handle. Undue delays at loading and unloading points must be minimized. Information obtained from actual operating experience should be used when planning for lighter employment in beach operations or high-speed vessel operations in ship-to-shore or shore-to-shore operations. If information is not available, factors noted in this manual may be helpful.

4-2.   The Transportation Theater Opening Element (TTOE) is essential during this process. The TTOE deploys early into the theater of operation to provide staff augmentation for planning reach-back capability, network visibility, joint reception, staging, onward movement (RSO) operations including life support, force protection, and theater sustainment operations. The TTOE becomes fully integrated into the staff of the headquarters to which attached to provide the commander with technical staff expertise for the planning and employment of transportation organizations engaged in theater and port opening operations. The TTOE is normally assigned to a theater sustainment command (TSC), attached to the sustainment brigade designated to conduct theater and port opening operations. Throughout the planning phase, the terminal commander appraises the situation based on directives and information from higher headquarters, the TTOE, his or her staff and the vessel masters involved in the operation. The appraisals decide the most effective use of Army watercraft. On the commander's final decision, the staff members prepare a detailed plan of operation. The operation plan covers all units assigned or attached to the terminal. It details the preparation and actual movement of vessel units. The appropriate terminal command plans the detailed operations of the attached vessel units at the site. The Harbormaster detachment provides a central control cell for all watercraft in the operating area and provides a common operating picture (COP) for the combatant commander.

4-3.   Preliminary rehearsal of units participating in watercraft cargo operations must occur prior to an actual operation and include all aspects, such as 1) Maneuvering vessels in close quarters, 2) Conducting beach, ship, and causeway approaches, 3) Material Handling Equipment operations (cranes and forklifts), 4) Floating crane operations (in port and anchored), and 5) Loading and discharging cargo and vehicles on vessels.

4-4.   The terminal command's operation plan includes items such as fuel and maintenance support as well as:

● Planned bivouacs and anchorages.

● Refueling and resupply plans and facilities, to include hazardous waste disposal.

● Communications instructions.

● Location and operations support units such as the maintenance company and Harbormaster Detachment Salvage capabilities.

● Threat assessment/Force Protection Conditions.

4-5.   The operation order must be clear and simple. Detailed alternate plans are prepared in case the operation plan proves infeasible. The terminal command or higher headquarters provides subordinate vessel units with various aids useful in planning and during operations. These may include–

● Aerial photographs - Beach reports based on interpretation of aerial photographs. (Photographs taken at low tide are preferred when showing the foreshore).

● Intelligence & planning tools with imbedded survey data.

● Beach reports provided by an Engineer Dive Team.

● Reliefs, surface models, other maps, digital products, charts, shoreline sketches, and photographs of the beach area, with as much detail as possible.

● Special studies prepared by theater intelligence agencies or other agencies (see Appendix A for an example of essential elements of information).

● Terrain studies and other reports from various informed sources.

4-6.   One of the most useful sources of information about the area of operations is the essential elements of information (EEI Appendix for a format). Issued by the terminal command or a higher headquarters, it is often distributed early in the planning phase as a reference for subordinate units. The area of planned operations directly influences the way watercraft are employed. See the Logistics over the Shore (LOTS) and Terminal Operations chapters for additional planning factors for special types of water transport operations.

PLANS AND ORDERS

4-7.   Plans and orders are based on those of the terminal command or other higher headquarters controlling the operation. The Transportation Theater Opening Element (TTOE) provides guidance on vessel operations at Echelons above Brigade. The plans must be sufficiently detailed so the subordinate units will not have to prepare extensive operation orders. Navigational plans must be carefully studied. Particular attention must be given to accuracy of time and distance calculations. Orders or instructions issued to subordinate vessel units will give detailed information about courses, tides, currents, communications, fuel, food for crews and passengers, assembly points, harbors of refuge, and defense against air or sea attacks. If the voyage is too short for adequate briefings aboard the craft, troops are briefed just before embarkation.

TASK ORGANIZATION

4-8.   Potential task organization for a water transport operation must take into consideration the capability of the area of operations to support and infrastructure. The deployed water transport task force and support element must be properly sized for the mission. A notional waterborne task force is shown in Figure 4-1.

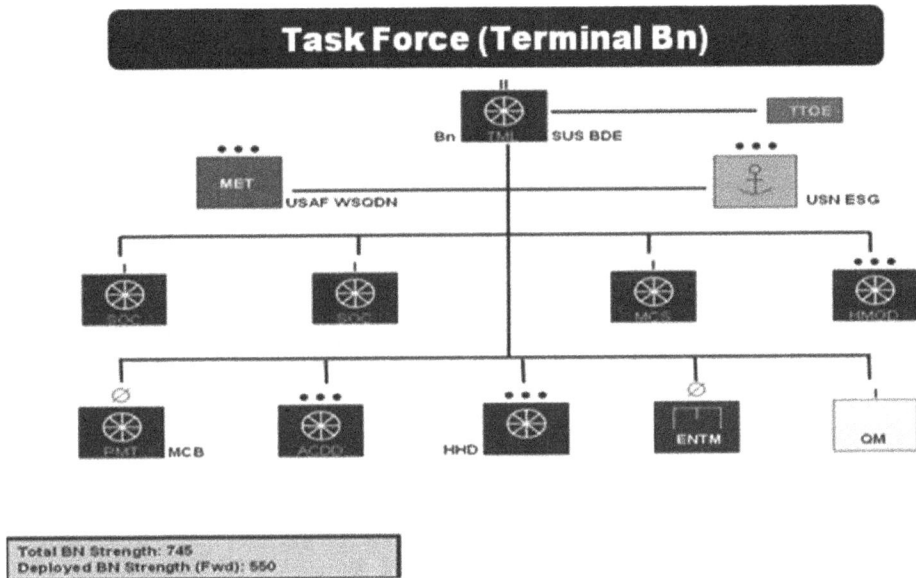

Figure 4-1. Example of a Water Transport Task Force configuration

Harbormaster Operations

4-9.   The Harbormaster Detachment is responsible for the coordinating and synchronizing vessel operations and proper functioning of the vessel. Usually, the Harbormaster Detachment goes ashore in one of the first vessels scheduled to land. They may also arrive, or send a section, as an advance party prior to vessel arrival. HMOD conduct a ground reconnaissance of the landing beach, check the actual conditions against plans, and make any necessary changes or modifications. A section of the Harbormaster Detachment lands in the first wave near the center of the beach and immediately erects range markers and other landing aids. When the remainder of the Detachment arrives, it establishes the Harbormaster Command and Control Center and the necessary radio communications and weather data sensors. The duties of the section on shore include:

- Helping to detect and remove underwater obstacles and other hazards to navigation.

- Marking obstacles that cannot be removed.

- Controlling and tracking vessel traffic during the approach of craft to the beach, while at the beach, and during departure from the beach.

- Coordinating emergency repairs to vessels.

- Coordinating salvage of vehicles that may become damaged or stalled in the water at the beach.

- Helping to evacuate casualties according to the medical plan (in a tactical landing).

- Help keep the beach clear.

- Communicating with vessels.

MEDICAL EVACUATION

4-10. One vessel should be designated for evacuation in event of a medical emergency. This is usually an LCM8 Mod 2, or similar craft. Procedures must be established and disseminated to all units. During mission rehearsals, notifications to support elements and transfer procedures are practiced. Ambulances must be located within the vicinity of the landing area, alert to assist where needed, or they may be embarked on a vessel for rapid dispatch to the anchored craft. Airborne Medical Evacuation (MEDEVAC) support is coordinated for remote or austere mission areas.

VESSEL COMMUNICATIONS

4-11. Communications are vital for water transport operations Ship-to-ship and ship-to-shore communications can be by data, satellite, radio, radiotelephone, flag hoist, and blinker signal lights (using Morse code). Shipboard communications are essential in normal water transport operations, combat support operations, distress situations, and/or sea-air rescue missions. Ships must be able to communicate across not only services, but international fleets.

4-12. The Global Maritime Distress and Safety System (GMDSS) suite provides distress and Search and Rescue communications capability. The Communications, Electronics & Navigation (CEN) equipment provides secure/non-secure, high to very high frequency (HF to VHF), short- and long-range communications capability appropriate for the mission capability of Army watercraft.

4-13. Army shipboard tactical communications can interface with Army land-based communications, Joint Navy, MSC, USCG, and merchant marine stations (shore and ship) and Military Affiliated Radio Stations (MARS) that will be used in joint operations, deployment, morale/welfare, and long-range missions. The signal systems aboard Army watercraft vary in type and design. These systems must meet Army tactical communications requirements and federal regulations that govern vessel communications.

COMMUNICATIONS TRAINING

4-14. Vessel watch-standers and radio operators must be thoroughly familiar with their communications equipment and procedures for initiating and conducting communications with civilian, commercial, and military operated vessels. Procedures may not be the same for communicating with merchant vessels as for military vessels, and can vary from informal bridge-to-bridge radio traffic to use of the Defense Messaging System (DMS) via Secure Internet Protocol Network (SIPRNET). All military mariners should be familiar with use of Allied Communications Publications (ACP).

4-15. Support personnel, such as communications equipment maintainers and specialized operators (25-series MOS) should be trained in the special requirements of maritime C4I, including operations and field maintenance of CEN equipment on vessels. Signal maintainers and operators should be assigned or attached to vessel units or field maintenance units, such as the Transportation Watercraft Maintenance Company, in order to best serve the maritime fleet's communications requirements.

TACTICAL COMMUNICATIONS

4-16. Tactical radios communicate with higher headquarters, other Army vessels, and military units that are being supported. FM 55-501 contains additional information on the various types of tactical radios used aboard Army vessels. Detailed information on a specific radio used for tactical communications is in the applicable TM for that particular system.

4-17. Code of Federal Regulations 47, Chapter 1, Part 80 delineates specific limitations and capabilities for marine communications, particularly GMDSS. Several radio systems are installed on Army vessels to meet the federal requirements for communications at sea. In addition, portable, handheld radios are used for internal shipboard communication, as well as local, short-range ship-to-ship, ship-to-shore, and detached work boat communications. Military research, development, and acquisition agencies are working together to reduce the cost of signal systems. They have determined that purchasing commercially designed radios that meet military requirements can save money and provide high tech, state-of-the-art signal systems that meet federal communication regulation requirements for vessels. As a result, different signal systems may be on Army vessels such as those described below.

Bridge-to-Bridge Radiotelephone

4-18. Commonly called bridge-to-bridge, this Very High Frequency (VHF) radiotelephone is part of the GMDSS requirement, and is designed to communicate between ships and from ship to shore.

Digital Selective Calling (DSC)

4-19. The Digital Selective Calling (DSC) capability is the primary capability within GMDSS, and provides the latest technology to Army watercraft communications. It adds an additional capability to the bridge-to-bridge radiotelephone. The system provides the vessel master with 200 different communication call functions and is equipped with built-in test equipment. Digital distress calling is provided on all DSC-equipped systems.

High-Frequency Radio Systems

4-20. The high-frequency (HF) systems give Army vessels the capability to communicate over great distances. They can be used in both secure and non-secure modes. There are several HF capabilities required, to support the missions of Army watercraft today. HF transceiver system can be operated double sideband and/or upper or lower sideband (USB/LSB), and should operate HF and VHF as required for the mission. It is designed as a continuous duty, high-frequency, single sideband transceiver.

International Maritime Satellite Systems (INMARSAT)

4-21. Maritime communications capabilities include satellite communications, especially INMARSAT, to be installed on each Army vessel. INMARSAT installation includes a stabilized tracking 85- to 100-centimeter dish antenna with radome and antenna cabling. Below decks equipment includes transceiver, processor, telephone, and telex units. An auxiliary receiver tuned to the Armed Forces Radio and Television Service (AFRTS) broadcast frequency and connected to the INMARSAT SES is also available. A public automatic branch exchange (PABX) is provided to furnish additional phone and data line connections to the Ship Earth Station (SES) if desired.

Configuration Management

4-22. Communications, Electronics, and Navigation (CEN) equipment on Army vessels is managed by Product Director, Army Watercraft Systems (PD-AWS) and other program offices. Vessel masters and unit Commanders must inventory and manage CEN to insure unauthorized changes are avoided.

4-23. Software for authorized applications must be kept on the vessel or at the unit to insure it is available for updates and program reloading if required.

4-24. Additional requirements for CEN, including satellite communications, electronic charting systems, Internet routers, wireless computer routers, etc. can be identified by users and supported units, but must not be incorporated on vessels without program office oversight.

4-25. Many capabilities are available that provide additional utility for successful mission accomplishment. Using the Department of Defense acquisition system to acquire these capabilities will insure safety, security, and interoperability are not compromised with addition of unauthorized systems.

PLANNING TIME FACTORS

4-26. Turnaround time is the basic factor to determine watercraft capabilities and requirements. It is used to compute the number of craft for a specific operation or the amount of tonnage that a given number of craft can deliver. Turnaround time is the total elapsed time that a single vessel takes to load, travel to the discharge point, unload, and return to shipside or terminal ready to be loaded again. The elements involved are average speed in the water, distance to be traveled, loading time, unloading time, and predictable delays. An estimated turnaround time must be worked out for each new operational site and mission and for each change in any of the elements given above. Sea, wind, and terrain conditions affect speed, and variations in loads alter loading and unloading times.

4-27. Average turnaround time is computed by using the following formula:

Turnaround time in hours = (round trip water distance in nautical miles/water speed in knots) + loading time in hours + unloading time in hours + potential delays in hours.

VESSEL REQUIREMENTS

4-28. Once an average turnaround time is established the number of vessels required to deliver an assigned daily tonnage can be computed by using the following formula:

Number of vessels required = (daily tonnage/average # tons per vessel) x (turnaround time in hours/hours of operation daily).

DAILY TONNAGE CAPABILITIES

4-29. Sometimes it is necessary to forecast the amount of tonnage that the available craft can transport over a specified period of time under existing conditions. Daily tonnage capabilities are computed by using the following formula.

4-30. Daily tonnage capability = (hours per operational day/turnaround time for vessel in hours) x (average tonnage per vessels x number of vessels available).

4-31. Commanders and staffs of vessel units must carefully study charts, maps, and port guides - focusing on the port channel and beach approaches, hydrographic information, and terrain as they affect vessel operations. The operations officer secures or prepares additional aids, if required, and. ensures the information is known and compatible for charts, maps, and global positioning systems in use.

4-32. As soon as the mission is received, the intelligence officer (S2) determines the requirements of the commanders and staffs for additional information. The S2 immediately initiates requests to the appropriate headquarters to obtain information as well as any maps, charts, or other planning aids that may be required. The commander of the vessel unit must secure as much detail as possible about the proposed landing beaches and how to approach them. Reconnaissance provides much of this information. Additional information is in intelligence documents and various publications distributed by higher headquarters. The battalion headquarters must ensure that all units are adequately supplied with maps and charts about the area of operations. The following types of nautical charts are used:

- Sailing charts are used to fix a position in long-distance navigation. They can employ Mercator's projection or Gnomonic projection for Great Circle sailing. Scales are 1:6,000,000 and smaller.

- General charts of the coast are used the same as sailing charts and also for near- shore navigation. They employ Mercator's projection. Scales are from 1:150,000 to 1:600,000.

4-33. Coast charts are used for coastwise navigation and to approach a shore from a long distance offshore. They show limited terrain contour lines details of land formations and artificial landmarks which help fix positions. Scales are 1:50,000 to 1:150,000.

4-34. Harbor/approach charts are used to navigate harbors and their approaches. They show greater detail of harbor natural and artificial features as well as the existence of hazards and/or routes of safe approach to the harbor. Scales are usually larger than 1:50,000.

WEATHER PLANNING

4-35. Whenever possible, vessel operations should be planned to take advantage of the best weather conditions. Appropriate weather activities should be requested to provide 24-hour forecasts every 12 hours along the intended route, commencing 24 to 36 hours before vessel departure and continuing until arrival. Requests for special weather forecasts should include the intended route and estimated speed. If internet access is available, weather data should be checked frequently along the route.

VESSEL CONTROL SYSTEM

4-36. Watercraft units must respond to the needs of the port operating units handling the cargo at shipside and at the beach. To maintain a smooth and continual flow of cargo over the beach, the watercraft unit commander must be aware of the status and location of his craft. This allows him to relocate platoons, sections, and individual vessels or to assign new or additional missions as rapidly as possible. Flexibility of operations requires a responsive, closely monitored control system. Control, maintained mainly by radio communication, is exercised through the harbormaster command & control center with remotely placed subordinate or partner control cells along various points on the beach and at shipside. The extent of the control system depends on the size of the operational area, the dispersion required, the ship-to-shore distance to be traveled, and the type of lighters being used. A typical control system includes 1) a main, centralized lighter control center (LCC) ashore, 2) A ship lighterage control point (SLCP) on each ship being worked and 3) A beach lighterage control point (BLCP) where the cargo is discharged.

USE OF CARGO HANDLERS

4-37. Aboard small lighters, crew members normally perform all shipside cargo-handling operations. If crew members are operating or maintaining their craft and cannot be spared for cargo handling duties, the terminal or unit commander may provide extra crewmen (commonly called "jumpers" from their capability to jump from vessel to vessel), to position and secure cargo in the vessel for movement between ports or from the ship to the beach. Aboard larger lighters, such as LCUs, a forklift is the most prompt method to position and stack unitized or palletized cargo. Port operating units provide and operates forklifts. Because transferring personnel from one craft to another alongside the ship is potentially hazardous, jumpers and forklift operators should board and debark the lighter at the port or beach and wear personal floatation devices (PFDs) and required safety gear while aboard the vessel.

CARGO DOCUMENTATION AND TRACKING

4-38. Cargo documentation is a function of the cargo documentation detachment. The commander of the lighterage unit determines from the terminal commander if there is a requirement to document the cargo in the ship-to-shore operation. If the requirement exists to assure in-transit visibility and to protect the audit trail, the commander of the lighterage is responsible for the cargo loaded aboard lighterage until it is unloaded at the discharge point.

4-39. If required, cargo is documented according to DOD 4500.9-R, Defense Transportation Regulation. The basic document for cargo movements under these procedures is DD Form 1384 (Transportation Control and Movement Document [TCMD]). This form is used as a dock receipt, a cargo delivery receipt, an accountability document during temporary holding, and a record of all cargo handled. The craft operator receives copies of the TCMD at shipside. The number of copies depends on command requirements for each particular discharge operation. The lighter operator signs for the cargo at shipside and delivers all copies, except one, to the shore side checker at the discharge point. The retained copy is initialed by the shore checker to indicate receipt of the cargo. At the end of the shift, the lighter operator turns in all initialed copies of the TCMD to the lighter control center. The information from these TCMDs provides the lighterage company with throughput evaluation data.

4-40. Cargo accountability may also be accomplished electronically using computer hardware and a 2½ by 2-inch Logistics Applications of Automated Marking and Reading Symbology (LOGMARS). A handheld portable bar code reader scans the cargo as it comes aboard the lighterage. The scanner works like an automated supermarket checkout counter. Once marked using Radio Frequency Identification (RFID) technology, the cargo can then be tracked worldwide by the Movement Tracking System (MTS). The cargo is scanned again when it is discharged. No paper documents the move, but the lighter operator can use the LOGMARS label to identify cargo.

PORT AREA SECURITY

4-41. The terminal commander is responsible for local defense of his portion of the operational area, and for ensuring adequate linkage to off shore and/or port security operations and communications with units executing those missions. There are special rules of engagement for cooperating with friendly forces during an engagement, and all commanders should insure their soldiers are properly trained in local Rules of Engagement (ROE). Commanders of all units have their normal responsibility for the security of personnel and equipment. Each unit is assigned a mission in the defense system. Emergency assembly areas are designated, an alert warning system is established. An overlay of the port or beach defense is circulated to all units in the area. Specific vessel defense measures are identified in Chapter 6 of this manual. General security measures taken by watercraft units within their bivouac areas include–

- Dispersing all vehicles, equipment, and personnel.

- Posting guards, patrols, and sentries.

- Constructing individual fighting position crew-served weapons, emplacements, communication trenches, and bunkers.

- Designating specific defense positions for all personnel and conducting alert drills to ensure personnel are familiar with their duties in an emergency.

- Organizing definite defense groups under leaders specifically designated in a published defense plan.

- Organizing communication systems to be used during defense operations.

- Constructing obstacles to prevent the advance of attacking forces.

- Planning for integrated fields of fire.

- Requesting Host Nation Support.

4-42. In an emergency, all members of the lighterage units, including vessel crews, may need to occupy defense positions. Accordingly, weapons must be kept handy at all times and checked frequently to ensure they are in serviceable condition. Defense plans for beach areas are coordinated with higher headquarters and integrated with other existing base defense plans to ensure mutual support. The responsible terminal headquarters establishes and coordinates normal passive and active security measures to protect the beach in an air attack. These measures consist mainly of concealment, dispersion, early warning, and weapons firing. Personnel are provided shelters. A system of alert warning signals is set up, and installations are camouflaged. Military police advises commanders on ways to secure and protect beaches against enemy threat. Exposed to pilferage and sabotage, beach areas become even more vulnerable to both enemy and criminal activities because of the accumulation of supplies. Military police become proactive to security requirements as threat activity increases.

4-43. Mines are one of the greatest threats watercraft may encounter in any type of operation. Of main concern to Army watercraft are the many varieties of shallow water, magnetic influence, and bottom mines. Surface ships, submarines, or aircraft can deliver these mines. With current capabilities including delayed arming devices and ship counters, the bottom mine poses a threat to watercraft during any phase of operations on the water. The bottom mine is also extremely difficult to detect on rocky bottoms or when buried in mud or silt. A buried mine loses none of its target acquisition or destruction capability. Mine hunting or sweeping platforms are intensively managed resources in any theater of operations. Potential sources for mine clearance services include the US Army divers, the US Navy, and the host nation. Mine and subsurface obstacle detection and counter-employment technologies must be developed and incorporated aboard vessels to insure high-payoff targets such as personnel and cargo-filled watercraft are provided early warning of danger and capability to protect vessel and payload.

PLANNING SEQUENCE

4-44. Water transport operations require detailed planning at all levels and close coordination with supporting elements. Units conducting water transport operations must be ready to begin as soon as possible after receiving orders. Preliminary training of units participating in riverine operations must occur prior to an actual operation and include all aspects, such as vessel operations, including maneuvering vessels in close quarters, loading and discharging cargo and vehicles on vessels, Material Handling Equipment operations (cranes and forklifts), Floating crane operations (in port and anchored) and security at the landing area.

4-45. Plans for water transport operations must be detailed enough to give all participating units complete information. Yet, they must be simple and flexible enough to be modified as the tactical situation changes. Plans for a water transport operation are usually developed in the following sequence:

- Scheme of maneuver based on METT-TC.

- Assault plan based on the scheme of maneuver.

- Water movement plan based on the assault plan and the scheme of maneuver. (The water movement plan includes composition of the water transport force, organization of movement serials, formation to be used, movement routes, command and control measures, mine countermeasures, plans for fire support, and immediate reaction to ambush.).

- Loading plan based on the water movement plan, the assault plan, vessel capabilities, and the scheme of maneuver.

- Marshaling plan, when required based on the loading plan, the water movement plan, the assault plan, and the scheme of maneuver.

- Deception plan, when required, based on the mission.

- Communications plan.

WATER TRANSPORT WITHDRAWAL

4-46. While preparing for water transport operations, planners determine the availability of waterways in the area of operations, the tide and current for the scheduled period of the operation, and suitable loading sites. This information, kept current during the operation, is the basis for planning the water transport withdrawal. Active employment of watercraft during an offensive maneuver simplifies deception in the initial stages of a water transport withdrawal. The quantity of available hydrographic information increases as a result of this employment. When possible, water transport withdrawal is timed so watercraft can approach loading areas with the current on the rising tide, load during slack high water, and depart with the current on the falling tide. Due to the security problems that accompany large water transport movements and using predictable routes, loading during the last hours of daylight and moving during darkness should be considered. Moving reconnaissance forward along possible withdrawal routes several hours ahead of the movement group is a useful deception measure. Loading, normally the most critical phase of the withdrawal requires detailed planning when selecting troop assembly areas, loading areas, loading control measures, and watercraft rendezvous areas.

SUMMARY

4-47. Successful planning of water transport operations requires expertise and experience. Senior personnel with this type of experience are imbedded in Theater Support Command Sea-Cells for this purpose. Land combatant commanders should leverage the expertise available to them by requesting planning support for operations requiring maneuver of combat forces across and through the maritime domain.

Chapter 5

Risk Management for Watercraft Operations

Accidents significantly reduce mission capabilities. Army must be prepared to operate worldwide in many watercraft environments, the watercraft mission has become increasingly demanding and so have its inherent risks. This increase in risk requires leaders to balance mission needs with hazards involved and to make wise risk decisions. Risk is the possibility of a loss combined with the probability of an occurrence. The loss can be death, injury, property damage, or mission failure. Composite risk management (CRM) identifies risks associated with a particular operation and weighs these risks against the overall training value to be gained. Principles of CRM are required to be applied to Watercraft by AR 385-10, Chapter 22 and applied to operations around the water by DA Pam 385-10.

NOTE: A low probability of an accident and an expected minor injury equals low risk. A high probability of an accident and an expected fatality equals high risk.

ELEMENTS

5-1.   Assessing risks has no hard and fast rules or formats. For example, pre-sail orders and inspections are essentially an assessment of risk. Different missions involve different elements that can affect operational safety. However, six elements are central to safely completing most missions: Planning, Supervision, Soldier selection, Soldier endurance, Weather, and Mission essential equipment.

5-2.   Using matrices that assign a risk level to each of the elements is one way to quickly assess the overall risks. The following matrices are examples of risk assessments for the seven elements common to watercraft missions.

NOTE: The factors are arbitrarily weighted. Modify them based on your particular mission and unit.

EXAMPLE: A landing craft ordered to make a dry ramp landing on a beach that had not been surveyed for gradient and underwater obstructions would create a high risk situation.

5-3.   Measure supervision risk by comparing command and control to the mission environment.

EXAMPLE: Your vessel has been placed under operational control of a Navy unit. You cannot adequately communicate with the Navy unit because of equipment incompatibility and communication procedures. In a night tactical environment, the risk becomes high.

5-4.   Measure soldier selection risk by comparing task complexity with soldier experience.

EXAMPLE: You are the master operating an LCU with no mate on board in restricted waters. If you leave the bridge, you place the vessel at high risk.

5-5.   Measure soldier endurance risk by comparing the mission environment with availability of basic needs (that is, rest, food, and water).

EXAMPLE: You are the master on an LSV operating in coastal waters with a crew shortage that does not allow for adequate crew rest. This places your vessel at high risk.

5-6.   Measure mission environment risk by comparing the level of supervision to the task location.

EXAMPLE: You are operating a causeway ferry (CF) during a LOTS operation off the coast. Severe weather is moving in. Safe haven is four hours away, but you have been released only two hours before the weather hits. This places your vessel at high risk.

5-7.   Measure equipment risk by comparing the availability of mission essential equipment with the readiness of that equipment.

EXAMPLE: You are an operator of an LMC-8 carrying very important persons during a LOTS operation. You do not have an enough life jackets for personnel on board. This places the crew and passengers at high risk.

5-8.   After assessing all the risks, the overall risk value equals the highest risk identified for anyone element. Next, focus on high risk elements and develop controls to reduce risks to an acceptable level. Control examples may include more planning; changes in location, supervision, personnel, or equipment; or waiting for better weather.

DECISION LEVEL

5-9.   The level of the decision maker should correspond to the level of the risk. The greater the risk, the more senior the final decision maker should be. Medium risk training warrants complete unit command involvement. If the risk level cannot be reduced, the company commander should decide to train or defer the mission. Operations with a high risk value warrant battalion involvement. If the risk level cannot be reduced, the battalion commander should decide to train or defer the mission. However, vessel masters aboard Army watercraft that are under way must sometimes make high risk decisions based on their judgment of the situation. A mission that was assessed at medium risk may suddenly become high risk, due to sudden changes in mission or weather situations. The table of Watercraft Risk Impact in Chapter 5 should be used to assist the leader in making weather index decisions.

RISK-CONTROL ALTERNATIVES

5-10.   The following options can help control risk:

*   Eliminate the hazard totally, if possible, or substitute a less hazardous alternative.

*   Reduce the magnitude of the hazard by changing tasks, locations, or times.

*   Modify operational procedures to minimize risk exposure consistent with mission needs.

*   Train and motivate personnel to perform to standards to avoid hazards.

SUPERVISION

5-11.   Leaders must monitor the operation to ensure risk control measures are followed. Never underestimate subordinates' abilities to sidetrack a decision they do not understand or support. Monitor the impact of risk reduction procedures when they are implemented to see that they really work, especially for new, untested procedures.

RESULTS

5-12. Risk management gives you the flexibility to modify your mission and environment while retaining essential mission values. Risk management is consistent with METT-TC decision processes and can be used in battle to increase mission effectiveness.

This page intentionally left blank.

Chapter 6

Vessel Security and Protection

The purpose of this chapter is to provide information about protection from threats to Army Watercraft that will assist commanders, vessel masters and coxswains with creating and implementing effective port and vessel security and protection programs with development of Pre-Planned Responses (PPR).

Adversaries are likely to conduct force projection denial operations by attacking Air and Sea Ports of Embarkation or Debarkation (APOEs/APODs and SPOEs/SPODs) as well as power projection platforms. If successful in slowing the operational tempo, the enemy will then seek asymmetrical means to counter-attack.

The US will most likely face future adversaries on a battlefield that includes urban and complex terrain, including along the littorals. The potential for a high-intensity major regional crisis requiring combat operations appears highly probable in the near future, and small-scale contingencies also are likely to continue to occur. The Army must therefore be ready to fight against any foe, regardless of the environment or scale of conflict.

This chapter provides guidance to:

- Establish and maintain watercraft unit security and protection programs that deter, detect, defend, mitigate and recover from the consequences of enemy attacks via the implementation of coherent baseline security measures.

- Defeat an attack by the activation of preplanned responses for watercraft crews.

OVERVIEW OF LESSONS LEARNED

6-1.   Military personnel, facilities, vessels, and material, are identifiable symbols of the U.S. Government, and are choice targets for enemies seeking to influence U.S. government policies at home or abroad.

6-2.   Protection of military assets is an Army core competency and therefore a critical part of every mission area. Planning for all operations include considerations for security and protection in order to maintain the readiness and effectiveness of Army forces. These efforts must not preclude unit mission. Watercraft unit commanders should be familiar with available resources for protecting ports, platforms and lines of communication and tailor the watercraft-specific Tactics, Techniques and Procedures (TTP) provided in this chapter and guidance from FM 3-37, *Protection*, to their specific mission requirements, threats, and resources.

FORCE PROTECTION CONDITIONS ON WATERCRAFT

6-3.   Force protection conditions (FPCON) are a series of measures designed to increase the level of a unit's defense against enemy attacks. FPCONs are not aimed at specific threats, but are selected based on a combination of the following factors: Basic force protection conditions are outlined in detail in FM 3-37.

6-4.   Shipboard measures for each FPCON are found in Appendix C of this manual. The listed measures are the Department of Defense standard for ships and as such may be referred to when developing PPR that feed into the overall Army Vessel Force Protection Plans required for submission to the port authority for Army-operated vessels entering DOD-administered ports.

6-5.   Army commanders who understand that threat scenarios are not static will design flexibility in their security plans. Commanders who also maintain a workable balance among competing requirements – mission accomplishment, resource utilization and FPCON posture - will be positioned to execute the most successful port or vessel security operations within theater Rules of Engagement parameters.

PREPLANNED RESPONSES

OVERVIEW

6-6.   Developed, exercised actions and measures that are implemented to identify, track, assess, and neutralize enemy attacks are called Pre-Planned Responses (PPR). This chapter sets forth specific guidance for commanders and planners to develop PPR that will be effective mechanisms to counter enemy threats. An online Joint Anti-Terrorism Guide (JAT) is available as a tool to develop plans in accordance with Department of Defense Instruction (DODI) 2000.16 *Anti-Terrorism Standards* at: https://atep.dtic.mil/jatguide .

6-7.   Sea movement, especially aboard military vessels, may provide a false sense of security. Sea operations are certainly more secure than urban patrols; however, ships transiting through restricted waterways such as straits, harbors, or anchored off hostile coastlines are visible and high-risk targets. Crews of ships in harbors need to evaluate each new port and determine possible enemy actions and ship's force counteractions (such as using fire and steam hoses to repel attackers).

6-8.   Crew members must be aware of Host Nation Support (HNS) and responsibilities while in port or anchored in foreign national waters.

6-9.   In accordance with Army Regulation 56-9 *Watercraft*, the ship's master is solely responsible for the ship and all those embarked. As a minimum, the master:

- Establishes methods of embarkation and debarkation and watch/patrol activities.
- Identifies vital areas of the ship (for example, engine room, weapons storage, bridge), and assigns security guards as required by the FPCON.
- Coordinates above and below waterline responsibilities.
- Establishes a weapons and ammunition policy and appoints a reaction force (e.g., ships self-defense force, and security teams).
- Coordinates for additional land and waterside security in ports of call.
- Ensures all personnel involved are trained through exercises or drills.

6-10. Army watercraft face threats whether at sea or in port. Overall threats are provided in FM 3-37. Likely threats against U.S. Army watercraft assets include:

- Small craft armed with individual weapons.
- Deep draft vessels.
- Swimmers and mines (floating or submersed IEDs).
- Pedestrian-carried IEDs.
- Vehicle or vessel-borne IEDs.
- Aircraft (ultra-lights, rotary wing).
- Standoff attacks (snipers, missiles, torpedoes).
- Man-portable air defense system (MANPADS), shoulder-fired rockets.
- Chemical, Biological, Radiological, Nuclear & High-yield Explosives (CBRNE) attacks (covert or overt).

Note: Listing of potential threats is for informational purposes only. Order does not indicate either the likelihood of occurrence or the degree of severity.

6-11. Development of PPR provides capability to create Force Protection Plans for watercraft. PPR are required in message format for entering Navy ports.

6-12. All PPR are organized by principles that will focus deliberate thinking, by planning considerations that will guide their effective implementation, and by specific actions to take when interacting with or engaging potential threats. However, the material in this chapter should not be considered the only available PPR against enemy threats. Commanders must always look beyond checklists to think critically and dynamically about potential threats for each mission and for each potential area of vulnerability.

COUNTERMEASURES

6-13. Preplanned countermeasures to deter threat activities can include installing mechanical devices, varying modes of watch-stander behavior, and employing physical barriers. Effective countermeasures include employment of random security and protection measures such as:

- Roving security patrols (varying size, timing, and routes).
- Sentry watch rotations.
- Military Working Dog (MWD) teams at Entry Check Points (ECP).
- Emplace barriers, roadblocks, and entry mazes.
- Visibly display crew-served weapons and sentries.
- Properly equip sentries with night vision devices (NVDs), binoculars, thermal imagers, and other vision-enhancement and personnel detection gear to enhance their abilities to detect enemy activity.
- Ensure sentries receive training in detecting suspicious activities and operating vision-enhancement and personnel detection devices.
- Establish sentry posts so that all potential avenues of approach can be observed.

6-14. Although the above countermeasures do not comprise an exhaustive list of preplanned employment capabilities, they will assist personnel with consistently maintaining a vigilant stance. By proactively watching for suspicious activity, observers have the highest chance of deterring threats before attacks can occur.

ESCALATION OF FORCE (EOF)

6-15. Escalation of Force (EoF) principles assist Soldiers in the application of force consistent with Rules of Engagement (ROE) and mission accomplishment in the contemporary, complex operating environment. They guide Leaders in Military Decision Making Process (MDMP), training, rehearsals, and mission execution where the application of force is a critical element. EoF principles leverage available force options (lethal and nonlethal) to set the conditions for desired outcomes (commander's intent) while reducing unnecessary death and collateral damage during the application of force. Escalation of Force principles include:

- EoF principles are NOT limitations on self-defense, do NOT apply to Declared Hostile Forces, are NOT a substitute for, but are a part of, ROE.
- EoF principles further follow self-defense rules, may minimize the loss of life and unnecessary suffering, and are part of mission analysis.
- Escalation of Force is NOT a step by step process, but a range of options.

6-16. The inherent right of unit commanders to exercise self-defense in response to a hostile act or demonstrated hostile intent still applies in off-base situations or off-vessel in foreign areas.

6-17. The International Institute of Humanitarian Law has published a Rules of Engagement Handbook, available on the U.S. Naval War College website, to provide military and civilian leaders a common reference that reflects ROE practice from nations across the globe and specifically provides valuable ROE information for the multinational force commander. It contains detailed guidance for maritime ROE, and is recommended reading for Army mariners, who routinely operate in International waters.

Possible signaling procedures for a target not immediately positively identified as a hostile threat are (in no particular order).

Daylight signaling procedures – use of:

- Ship's horn.
- Loud speaker in local language.
- Flash-bang munitions.
- Signs in local language.
- Colored flags or paddles.
- Smoke Grenades.
- Hand and arm signals.

Night and limited visibility signaling procedures – use of:

- Spotlights.
- Laser pointers.
- Flash/bang munitions.
- Emergency vehicle lights.
- Flares.

SELF DEFENSE

6-18. **Unit self defense**. A unit commander has the authority and obligation to use all necessary means available and to take all appropriate actions to defend the unit, including elements and personnel, or other US forces in the vicinity, against a hostile act or demonstrated hostile intent. In defending against a hostile act or demonstrated hostile intent, unit commanders will use only that degree of force necessary to decisively counter the hostile act or demonstrated hostile intent and to ensure the continued protection of US forces (see subparagraph 8a of this enclosure for amplification).

6-19. **Individual Self-Defense.** Commanders have the obligation to ensure that individuals within their respective units are trained on and understand when and how to use force in self-defense.

ACTION IN SELF-DEFENSE

6-20. **Means of Self-Defense**. All necessary means available and all appropriate actions may be used in self-defense. The following guidelines apply for individual, unit, national, or collective self-defense:

- Attempt to De-Escalate the Situation. When time and circumstances permit, the hostile force should be warned and given the opportunity to withdraw or cease threatening actions (see Appendix A of this Enclosure for amplification).

- Use Proportional Force – Which May Include Nonlethal Weapons -- to Control the Situation. When the use of force in self-defense is necessary, the nature, duration, and scope of the engagement should not exceed that which is required to decisively counter the hostile act or demonstrated hostile intent and to ensure the continued protection of US forces or other protected personnel or property.

- Attack to Disable or Destroy. An attack to disable or destroy a hostile force is authorized when such action is the only prudent means by which a hostile act or demonstration of hostile intent can be prevented or terminated. When such conditions exist, engagement is authorized only while the hostile force continues to commit hostile acts or exhibit hostile intent.

NOTE: Use of nonlethal weapons provides a useful element of use of force that can prevent escalation of the situation without producing irrevocable fatalities. This is provided by fully developed and fully-understood rules of engagement that are backed by extensive training. As a matter of principle, non-lethal weapons should never be employed without adequate lethal support that is clearly displayed to the potential adversary. There must be no doubt in the mind of a potential aggressor that we possess sufficient force to accomplish the mission, and that we are prepared to use that force should the situation so dictate. Further, it should be clearly understood that our Soldiers are not required to use nonlethal force before employing lethal force.

VESSEL CREW ESCALATION OF FORCE (Sample Vignette):

1. The vessel master gains or maintains situational awareness (SA) using information that is gathered from vessel radar, Force XXI Battle Command Brigade and Below (FBCB2) (if applicable) movement tracking system (MTS), frequency modulated (FM) communications, maps or charts, intelligence summaries, situation reports (SITREPs), and or other available information sources.

2. The vessel master provides relevant information to the entire crew by radio, sound-powered phone, relay, verbal or hand and arm signals. All crew members share a common picture of the operating environment, via the vessel master's oversight and command. The vessel master communicates supporting fires requirements to designated support units and/or higher headquarters via the most expedient means, with the supporting units providing fire or air support.

3. All soldiers will immediately share information of a suspicious or potentially suspicious item, person(s), vessel, or vehicle with other members of the crew via any and all means necessary.

4. Crew responds with appropriate level of force in accordance with Rules of Engagement.

5. Vessel master will provide guidance and direction to crew members observing the potential threat to conduct further evaluation of intent and begin escalation of force. The Officer in Charge (OIC) on site will pass information up and down the chain to the vessel master, team members, or other unit as required.

EMPLOYMENT OF NON-LETHAL EFFECTS

6-21. **Non-Lethal Weapons (NLW) Definition**: Non-Lethal Weapons are defined as "Weapons, devices and munitions that are explicitly designed and primarily employed to immediately incapacitate targeted personnel or materiel, while minimizing fatalities, permanent injury to personnel, and undesired damage to property in the targeted area or environment. Non-lethal weapons are intended to have reversible effects on personnel or materiel."

6-22. Non-lethal capabilities are *never* limiting to the commanders' option to employ lethal force as the situation merits. They are an enabler for measured escalation of force, adaptable as situation merits.

6-23. If equipped with non-lethal effects, Army watercraft will adopt the TTPs found in FM 3-22.40, *Multi-Service Tactics, Techniques and Procedures for Tactical Employment of Non-Lethal Weapons*.

6-24. Non-lethal doctrine and policy provides guidance on incorporation of non-lethal effects as tools to achieve measured escalation of force to perform the mission while acting in accordance with Rules of Engagement (ROE).

SMALL CRAFT THREAT

6-25. As the bombing of the USS COLE in October 2000 clearly demonstrated, a small craft can be a lethal weapon. In a matter of minutes, a small craft carrying approximately 500 pounds of explosives approached the port side of the COLE, exploded, and left a gaping hole in the ship, causing the death of 17 sailors and many injuries.

SMALL CRAFT DETECTION PRINCIPLES

6-26. The purpose for developing PPR to counter small craft attacks is to prevent threats from gaining close proximity to protected assets or areas. The following principles, illustrated in Figure 6-1, will guide the development of PPR to counter a small craft threat:

- Detect and assess all vessels entering a predetermined assessment zone.
- Establish positive ID and determine hostile intent of all vessels in the warning zone. Non-lethal warning devices are ideal for this purpose.
- Prevent unauthorized vessels from entering the threat zone.
- Size of zone is determined by the vessel master in accordance with METT-TC.

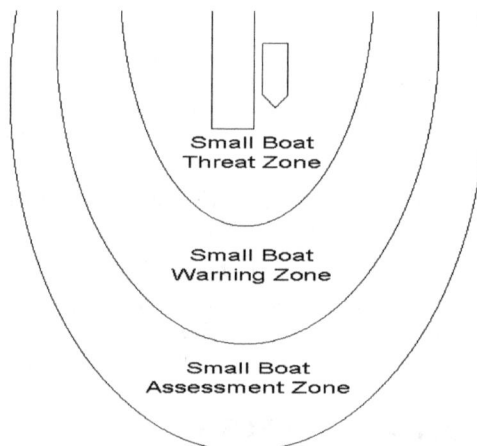

Figure 6-1. Small Craft Threat Zones

SMALL CRAFT DETECTION CONSIDERATIONS

6-27. Small craft threats are one of the most lethal methods of enemy attack. When developing PPR, use the FPCon appendix in this manual.

6-28. Any craft has the potential to be a threat, it is imperative to determine hostile intent, and neutralize any threats.

6-29. The continuum of force is a dynamic set of measures to be employed as the situation dictates. The following factors shape security force measures to determine hostile intent:

- Contact actions (e.g., display weapons, aggressively avoid security crafts, ignore warnings).
- Operating area (e.g., small zones limit time and distance to interact with contact).
- Security craft capabilities (e.g., underpowered craft cannot maneuver with contact).
- Restrictive ROE (e.g., cannot use warning shots).
- HN restrictions (e.g., only HN security forces can interact with civilian craft).
- Availability of Non-lethal effects and warning munitions.

DEEP DRAFT THREAT

6-30. The potential for deep draft ships to inflict devastating damage is due to their large capacity to hold explosives and to the difficulty friendly forces will face trying to stop an underway vessel.

6-31. Security forces and crafts can stop hostile small craft by shouldering, ramming or shooting them; while the same measures could be employed against an approaching hostile ship, the likelihood of stopping it is minimal. Additionally, some nations employ gunships that are much better-armed than Army vessels. Use of warning shots toward such a craft may be construed as hostile action, or used as an excuse to escalate the situation.

DEEP DRAFT THREAT PRINCIPLES

6-32. The following principles will guide commanders in forming PPR to counter a deep draft threat:

- Liaison with Navy, HN or USCG authorities and use common operational picture (COP) awareness tools to ensure all deep draft vessels in the area are tracked.
- Detect, assess, and determine hostile intent as far away from the protected asset or area as possible so security forces have time to react.
- Coordinate air fire support assets.

SUBSURFACE THREAT

6-33. The third water transport threat occurs at the subsurface level, carried out by either swimmers or mines, or a combination of the two. Both threats were used successfully during the Vietnam War and remain attractive enemy options because of their relatively low cost and simplicity. The most difficult aspect when planning to defend against subsurface threats is employment of capability to detect them. Small crafts and deep draft vessels are clearly visible and thus provide at least some time to determine hostile intent; security forces may not see a swimmer or mine until it is in the threat zone, if at all. While a mine is clearly a threat and should be acted upon immediately, a swimmer or bubbles in the water are not necessarily indicative of a hostile threat.

Subsurface detection technologies should be employed by shore and vessel units, especially if intelligence indicates subsurface threat employment is likely in the area of operations.

SUBSURFACE THREAT PRINCIPLES

6-34.   The following principles will guide the development of PPR to detect and deter subsurface threats:

● Develop specific guidance for reacting to a surfaced swimmer or bubbles sighting. Such directives are critical because of the likelihood that defenders will get only one look at the swimmer at the water surface. Is any swimmer in the water within a certain distance from the protected asset or area assumed to be hostile? Can concussion grenades automatically be used if a swimmer submerges or bubbles are seen? Pre-Planned Responses to these questions will ensure security forces are armed with sufficient authority to counter this elusive threat.

● Install barriers at a distance from the protected asset or area if there is a likely threat of mines.

● Use anti-swimmer devices when possible. A variety of commercial anti-swimmer products that either put sound into the water to deter a swimmer, or detect a swimmer with a variant of sonar are increasingly available to U.S. military maritime assets. Non-lethal anti-swimmer munitions may be employed.

AIRCRAFT THREAT

6-35. The short reaction time associated with most enemy attacks is further lessened when countering an aircraft attack. With so much focus on waterborne and land threats, aircraft may go unnoticed. If aircraft are deemed to be hostile and security forces open fire with weapons, there is the added concern of collateral damage from expended rounds. While this risk exists when firing on waterborne and land threats, the potential for collateral damage is greater when firing against an air threat.

AIRCRAFT THREAT PRINCIPLES

6-36. As definitively shown on 11 September 2001, aircraft can be used as a weapon or to deliver another weapon such as a bomb, missile or chemical/biological agent. Principles when developing PPR to counter an aircraft threat are as follows:

● Coordinate among all agencies dealing with control in the airspace around the protected asset or area so early assessment of hostile intent can be made.

● Visually assess all aircraft near protected assets or areas.

● Consider firing arcs and select weapons to minimize collateral damage. Responsible local air traffic control and U.S. units should warn suspected hostile aircraft. Noncompliance is not necessarily a hostile act, but if the aircraft continues on a collision course, the decision to engage should be made far enough out to be effective in stopping the potential attack. The ideal weapons for defense against aircraft threats are surface-to-air missiles and crew-served weapons. Although difficult to initially detect, small general aviation aircraft are relatively easy to destroy once hostile intent can be established. Army Watercraft may not have capability to determine aircraft hostile intent or employ anti-aircraft weapons. Passive defense measures should be coordinated for and employed when operating in identified high aircraft threat areas. Coordination should be established within the operational area for anti-aircraft threat support for Army Watercraft as required.

STANDOFF ATTACK THREAT

6-37. One of the most difficult threats to detect, deter, and defend against is a standoff attack, primarily because close contact is never made between the attacker and security forces. Distance and the likelihood that the threat is in a civilian or concealed area make eliminating the threat more hazardous. The most likely standoff threats are snipers, mortars, rocket-propelled grenades (RPGs), and man-portable air defense weapons such as a Stinger missile. Snipers use rifles as antipersonnel weapons, while mortars and RPGs are used primarily as anti equipment weapons.

STANDOFF ATTACK THREAT PRINCIPLES

6-38. The best way to defeat a standoff threat is to keep it from happening. Close cooperation with civilian or HN authorities to counter standoff attacks is essential. Principles that guide development of PPR against a standoff threat are:

- Lessen the number of potential targets by reducing the visibility of critical assets and areas.

- Extend watch standers' focus beyond the area immediately around the asset in order to assess potential standoff threats.

- Maintain a close liaison with civilian or HN authorities to quickly counter standoff threats.

MAN-PORTABLE AIR DEFENSE SYSTEM (MANPADS)

MAN-PORTABLE AIR DEFENSE SYSTEM THREAT

6-39. Potential damage and loss of life resulting from the employment of a MANPADS is greater than from a sniper or mortar threat. The November 2002 enemy attack on an Israeli airliner in Kenya highlights the potential anti air MANPADS threat to U.S. aviation assets. It is important that Army mariners be familiar with this threat, as the JHSV is capable of supporting shipboard aviation operations. Since MANPADS threats will typically launch a single missile as opposed to a recurring sniper or mortar threat, the key to countering the threat is to prevent its recurrence. Criteria to identify possible enemy MANPADS launch sites include:

- **Accessibility and concealment:** A location chosen for ease of ingress/egress and concealed enough to allow the hostile fire team to get into position, assemble the weapon, and fire it without being discovered by security force personnel.

- **Line of sight:** The need for a enemy to have an unobstructed view of the target.

- **Exposure time:** The amount of time the intended target is vulnerable from an operational attack.

- **Distance to target:** The distance required by a enemy to positively identify the intended target.

Summary

6-40. Commanders with watercraft units must plan for every aspect of operations, including protection of vessels, crews, passengers and cargo. Preplanned responses, when orchestrated, drilled, and resourced, will insure Army watercraft and other port assets are protected from most threats. Not every threat can be planned for or foreseen, but a trained crew will be capable of adapting and overcoming when those unforeseen events occur.

This page intentionally left blank.

Chapter 7

Logistics Over-The-Shore (LOTS) Operations

Loading and unloading of ocean going ships is faster and safer at a port complex. At times however, when deploying units from the sea, or when developed seaports are unavailable (denied) or damaged, unloading from offshore may be necessary. This is a potentially dangerous, highly weather dependent operation – one that should only be used with careful planning. However, it can greatly enhance capability to increase throughput into an area.

Logistics over the Shore (LOTS) are tailorable operations involving the movement of cargo from a ship anchored offshore to an improved or unimproved beach site. More specifically, cargo is transferred from a vessel to Army watercraft where it is then transported to shore, where the watercraft is offloaded. Anti-access strategies employed by adversaries may require widely scattered, point of need, beach and austere port operations instead of a large RSOI footprint in a single location.

SITE RECONNAISSANCE

7-1.   In follow-on LOTS operations, the joint force commander may be inclined to leverage beaches already selected by the Navy and the US Marine Corps (USMC) for the initial forcible entry phase of an operation. However, the beaches that best facilitate amphibious operations may not be advantageous for setting up LOTS operations. For most follow on LOTS operations, a new beach site will be selected that has the key characteristics of deeper gradient, hard-pan cargo marshalling areas, and access to existing infrastructure.

7-2.   A beach reconnaissance party determines the exact location of the site. The reconnaissance party consists of representatives of the SDDC Terminal Transportation Group, sustainment brigade, engineer support unit and the military police; the commander and the operations officer of the terminal battalion that will operate the site; and the commanders of the port operating units and vessel companies involved. During the reconnaissance, the Terminal Battalion commander selects and assigns company areas and frontages, indicates areas of defense responsibilities, and tentatively organizes the area of operations.

7-3.   The water transport unit commanders provide advice and recommendations on factors and conditions that affect their units. These recommendations bear directly on the final choice of the exact operational sites. When Chemical, Biological, Radiological, and Nuclear (CBRN) operations are suspected, the beach reconnaissance party conducts radiological monitoring, surveys, and chemical agent detection activities to determine possible contamination of prospective beach sites.

SITE SELECTION

7-4.   When planning to open new bare beach sites most advantageous for LOTS operations, the first step is to determine the beach areas available. The theater opening element selects the general operational area in coordination with the Navy and the Military Sealift Command.

7-5.   After the initial reconnaissance is completed and the terminal battalions have been dispersed to sites along the coastline, the commander must ensure that the battalions have the units, equipment, and other support needed for the assigned mission. Beaches ideally suited for LOTS without prior preparation or alteration are rare. Therefore, varying levels of engineering support is normally required to enable landing craft to beach and to provide exits from the beach to marshaling areas and the clearance transportation network. Each bare beach LOTS discharge point requires closest attention and the greatest coordination. The success of beach operations depends on the efficiency of cargo clearance. Supplies and equipment being brought to the beach must be cleared as rapidly as possible to inland destinations. This will prevent the buildup of cargo ("Iron Mountain") on the beach, thus eliminating or reducing targeting by the enemy and hindrances to cargo movement.

7-6.　Once a general area for LOTS operations has been identified, the next step is to select a beach site for each type activity (Figure 7-1).

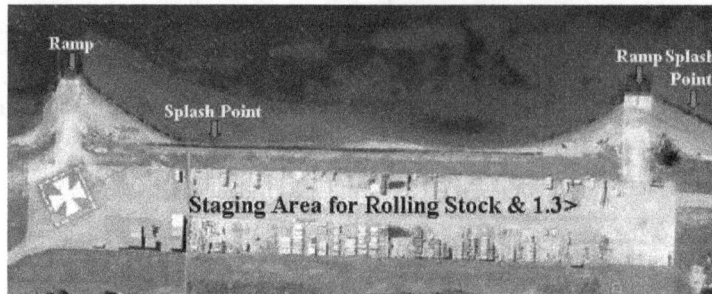

Figure 7-1. Cargo staging area

BEACH RECONNAISSANCE

7-7.　Selecting the beach site is an initial step in planning offshore discharge operations. Site selection must be in coordination with the Navy the Military Sealift Command. A reconnaissance party consisting of representatives of the Army, including the commander of the terminal battalion that will operate the site, the commanders of the cargo handling companies, and representatives of the units that will provide lighter support usually select the exact site.

7-8.　During the reconnaissance, the commander of the terminal battalion assigns company areas and beach frontages, indicates areas of defense responsibility, locates his temporary command post, and tentatively organizes the area for operational use. If a ground reconnaissance cannot be made, maps, aerial photographs, and information gathered from intelligence sources form the basis for a careful study of the operational area. If possible, the commanders and staff officers responsible for planning should perform an air reconnaissance of the area. Commanders and staffs of vessel units must make a detailed study of the terrain, hydrographic conditions, enemy capabilities and dispositions, civil population and attitude, and similarities between factors affecting vessel movements and approaches to the beach. They must also analyze the lighterage requirements and the tonnages to be handled by their craft.

7-9.　When selecting a specific area for beach operations, the water transport unit commander is particularly interested in the following physical and environmental characteristics.

7-10.　Beach Composition: Type of soil, beach gradient at various tide stages, and length and width of beach.

7-11.　Beaches are classified by their predominant surface material, such as silt, mud, sand, gravel, boulders, rock, or coral, or by combinations of sand and boulders. The ideal composition for beaching landing craft is a combination of sand and gravel. Silt, mud, or fine sand may clog the cooling system of landing craft. Rock, coral, or boulders may damage the hull or the underwater propulsion and steering mechanism. Firm sand provides a good beach traffic area for personnel and vehicles. A beach is usually firmest when it is damp and when the material is of small size. Gravel has good bearing capacity but poor shear strength. As a general rule, the coarser the material, the poorer the capacity to handle vehicle traffic.

7-12.　Beach gradient or underwater slope is usually expressed as a ratio of depth to horizontal distance. For example, a gradient of 1:50 indicates an increase in depth of 1 foot (.3048 meter) for every 50 feet (15.2

meters) of horizontal distance. For landing operations, it is usually necessary to find the gradient only from the water's edge seaward to a depth of 3 fathoms (5.5 meters).

7-13. Beach gradients are usually described as: Steep (more than 1:15), Moderate (1:15 to 1:30), Gentle (1:30 to 1:60), Mild (1:60 to 1:120), or Flat (less than 1:120).

7-14. Underwater gradients can seldom be determined from hydrographic charts. Only a few areas have charts scaled larger than 1:100,000. Moreover, since the inshore seabed is subject to frequent change, only a very recent survey would have any value. However, there are ways to estimate gradient.

7-15. Commanders and operational planners should gravitate to beach gradients that are moderate to gentle.

7-16. The ideal beach for landing craft operations is one with deep water close to shore, a firm bottom of hard-packed sand and gravel, minimum variation in tides, and a moderate to gentle (1:15 to 1:60) underwater beach gradient. It also has no underwater obstructions to seaward and no current or surf. Although such a beach will rarely exist in the area of operations, the battalion or unit commander weighs the characteristics of existing beaches against these desirable features.

OTHER CONSIDERATIONS

7-17. Shore water Composition: Depth of water close ashore, Tidal range and period (duration and variation of high and low water), effect of tides on the beach width.

7-18. Wind and weather conditions in the area (using Beaufort Scale).

7-19. Sea bottoms most nearly ideal for landing craft operations have coarse sand, shell, and gravel bottoms and similar foreshore beach composition. These bottoms are firm and usually smooth; but bank, bar, and shoal formations are common. Bottom compositions of soft mud or fine, loose sand can be hazardous to vessels, vehicles, and personnel. Soft mud and loose sand could foul the engine cooling systems. Crews on craft equipped with beaching tanks rely on this supply of cooling water during beaching operations to prevent engine fouling. Crews on vessels not equipped with beaching tanks must clean the sea strainers often to ensure the engine gets an adequate supply of cooling water.

7-20. Vehicles sink into beaches with a soft bottom and become immobilized. Mud and sand bottoms may be either firm or soft, depending on the percentage of sand. A mud bottom over a rock base may be satisfactory if the mud is not more than 1 or 2 feet (0.3 or 0.6 meters) deep. Coral heads, rocks, and other underwater obstructions in shallow waters near shore can cause bent propellers and shafts, broken skegs, and punctured hulls. Rocks covered with algae are extremely difficult for personnel to walk on and may cause wheeled vehicles to lose traction.

7-21. Sandbars are likely to develop offshore of long, sandy beaches that are exposed to continuous wave action. On aerial photographs of quiet sea and clear water, sandbars appear as a narrow band of light tone against a dark bottom. On photographs of rough water, sandbars are detected by a line of breakers outside the normal surf zone. A sandbar indicates a sandy bottom offshore and unless there are visible rock outcrops, probably a smooth, sandy bottom inshore of the bar. These characteristics, when accompanied by sand dunes behind the beach, indicate that the beach is mostly sand. Surf is likely on such beaches. The height of the surf can usually be estimated accurately under a given wind or sea swell condition if the approximate depth over the sandbar is known.

7-22. Sandbars can be a serious menace to landings. Craft may run hard aground on them while still some distance from the beach loading or discharge point. When this occurs and an appreciable sea is breaking on the bar, the craft may swamp and broach to. If troops debark while the craft is hung on a sandbar, they may be endangered due to depth of water, strong currents, or a soft bottom between the bar and the beach. Rather than be endangered, personnel should remain aboard the craft. Successive seas may lift the craft over the bar. Then the craft can proceed to the beach. If the sea condition permits and the craft is unlikely to free itself from the bar, personnel should be transferred to other craft if possible, and salvage begun to retrieve the craft. Tidal variations influence the times when beaching can be attempted.

7-23. Even though there may not be sandbars at a particular beach site or surf zone at the initial landing, the scouring action of the propellers of beached landing craft may create them. After several days, a built-up bar of this type may be large enough to prevent the satisfactory beaching of large landing craft and similar vessels. Alternating beaching sites reduces this hazard.

7-24. Small sandbars may be formed between runnels within the tidal range on foreshores having a slight slope. A runnel is a temporary small channel on the beach formed by water during normal tidal motion. A foreshore is the part of shore between the high water mark and low water mark.

7-25. The height of these bars is seldom more than 2 feet (0.6 meter) from the bottom of the trough to the top of the crest. However, such bars are hazardous to operations because landing craft may ground on the crests and troops and equipment must cross the stream of water to reach the dry shore. If the bottom of the runnel is silt, vehicles and heavy equipment may be unable to transit the beach. It may be necessary to beach the craft at high tide and unload it after the water has receded to a point where matting can be laid across the troughs. Whenever bars are present, the wave crests peak up as the waves roll over the bar. The water depth over the bar and the wave height determine if breaking takes place on or near the bar. If water depth over the bar is more than twice the significant breaker height, nearly all waves pass over the bar without breaking, but crests peak up distinctly. If the depth is between one and two times the breaker height, waves break near the bar, some on the bar itself, and others on the shoreward side. All waves break on the seaward side when the water depth over the bar is less than the breaker height. Frequently, more than one bar exists with waves breaking and re- forming and breaking again on another bar or on the beach.

7-26. High surf greatly modifies bar depth and distance from shore. There is a rough relationship between bar depth and the maximum breaker height during the preceding one or two weeks. If the breakers remain constant in height long enough, the bar attains a depth slightly less than the depth of breaking at low tide. Large waves do not ordinarily last long enough to cause this adjustment.

ROCKS

7-27. Rocks on a beach may limit the shore approaches so that only a few craft can land at once. This prevents a large-scale landing and restricts beach operations. However, one or two rocky patches fronting a beach do not present a serious obstacle. There is slight chance that craft will strike rocky patches that have been properly marked with buoys. In a heavy sea, waves break over rocky patches on the bottom. A light sea with waves breaking on the rocks indicates that the rocks are dangerously close to the surface.

REEFS

7-28. Coral reefs are found in shallow salt water in tropical areas. The three general types of reefs are identified below.

Fringing reefs. Fringing reefs that are attached to the land. The reef may be only a few feet wide and is seldom more than a mile wide. Inshore vessel channels are often present on fringing reefs, but they do not occur when the reef is narrow and exposed to heavy surf action. These vessel channels are about 1 to 5 feet (0.3 to 1.5 meters) deeper than the rest of the reef surface and may be 10 to 50 yards (9.1 to 45.7 meters) wide. These channels run parallel and close to the shore, open seaward through breaks in the reef, and may continue for a nautical mile (1.852 kilometers) or more. The channels trap sediment brought down from the land or shifted inshore from the seaward side of the reef. This sediment is often quite fine; giving the vessel channels a bottom of sand or mud, although clumps of coral may live in them. Generally, they are deep enough for the smaller landing craft and too deep for troops to wade.

Barrier Reefs. Barrier reefs lie offshore and are separated from the land by a lagoon. There may be a fringing reef on the land side of the barrier reef. Barrier reefs vary in width from a few hundred feet (meters) to more than a nautical mile (1.852 kilometers) and may have reef islands on them.

Atoll reefs. These barrier reefs enclose lagoons. They usually have a crescent shape with the convex side toward the sea. They may contain reef islands, or heads, composed of accumulated debris from the reef. These circular, drum like islands are seldom more than 10 to 15 feet (3.1 to 4.0 meters) higher than the reef flat. They may be up to 100 feet (30.5 meters) in diameter with a low, swampy interior. The water surrounding a coral island is usually smooth, and the island's presence may not be indicated by surf. However, the water changes color near the island from deep blue to light brown. The chief obstacles on the seaward side of an atoll reef are the marginal ridge with its consequent surf and the scattered boulders of the reef, which are difficult to spot. The inshore part of the reef is usually critical in landing operations. Often it is a band from 50 to 100 yards wide (45.7 to 91.4 meters) with boulders that may impede vehicular progress. On the whole, the surface of an atoll reef is more favorable for crossing than the surface of a fringing or barrier reef. On the lagoon side, the beaches are apt to be composed of softer sand than the seaward beaches. A landing on the lagoon side should be undertaken at high tide, and the numerous coral columns that grow in shallow water near the shore must be bypassed.

SEAWEED

7-29. Seaweed is usually found in calm waters. It may interfere with the operation of landing craft and wheeled or tracked amphibians. The marine growth may consist of free- floating minute particles that clog sea strainer intakes for engine cooling water, or it maybe a thick, heavy type of weed that fouls propellers and tracks.

CURRENTS

7-30. When visibility is poor, water currents of variable direction and low, changing velocity may interfere with or prevent landing at the designated point on a beach. When alongshore currents are anticipated, unmistakable markers or landmarks are needed to identify the beach and the approach lines. Even though landing craft compasses may be properly compensated the current and weather may prevent vessel operators from following the intended course. Therefore, all vessel operators must be aware of natural and artificial ranges that can be used to mark beach approaches during day and night operations. Directing individual craft by radio from a radar-equipped command and control vessel or from the vessel being discharged is a satisfactory method during reduced visibility.

7-31. A strong alongshore current may contribute to the broaching-to of craft. A broached-to condition exists when a craft is cast parallel to the current or surf and grounded such that maneuverability is greatly reduced. To prevent this condition, vessel operators must be extremely careful when approaching, retracting from, or trying to maintain a position on a beach. Broaching-to is dangerous if the surf is running since the craft can be swamped or driven higher onto the beach. In either case, assistance will probably be needed to recover the vessel. Unloading broached-to craft is difficult. Injury to personnel and damage to the craft and its cargo may result from attempts to remove cargo when the craft is not perpendicular to the surf or current. If there are very strong alongshore currents, the beach may become cluttered with broached-to and swamped vessels unless broaching lines are used or breakwaters and jetties are constructed.

7-32. Offshore and inshore currents are very important to watercraft operations. Offshore currents are found outside the surf zone. Tidal currents predominate around the entrances to bays and sounds, in channels between islands, or between an island and the mainland. Tidal currents generally change direction every 6 to 12 hours and may reach velocities of several knots in narrow sounds. On the surface, tidal currents may be visible as tide rips or as areas of broken water and white caps. Tidal currents are predictable; they repeat themselves as regularly as the tides to which they relate. Non-tidal currents are related to the distribution of density in the ocean and the effects of wind. Currents of this type are constant for long periods and vary in direction and velocity during different seasons. References are available for predicting area tidal currents.

SURF

7-33. Ocean waves arise as a result of local and offshore winds on the ocean surface. Two types of surface waves are produced: wind waves and swells. Wind waves are usually steep with a short time between successive crests. Frequently, the crests break in deep water. When crests are small, they are called whitecaps. When crests are large, they are called combers or breaking seas. In deep water, these waves seriously affect the performance of small craft. Swells result from storms great distances from the coast. They are characterized by a long, smooth undulation of the sea surface. These waves never break in deep water, and time between successive crests may be very long. Small craft in deep water are not affected by swell; however, swell does cause larger vessels to roll and pitch in deep water. In shallow water, swells increase in height. Upon reaching a sufficiently shallow depth, swells may give rise to an immense surf that may damage shore installations or make harbor entrances impassable.

7-34. Swell arising from distant storms approaches the coast at high speeds. In the case of a large offshore disturbance, the swell usually arrives at the shoreline ahead of the storm. For this reason, vessels trying to reach harbors ahead of a storm may find the entrance impassable due to breaking swell.

7-35. The angle at which waves break in respect to shoreline contours generates a number of complications to landing craft operations. To successfully traverse the surf zone, landing craft must first estimate the direction and total distance of drift and then direct a course so that the craft meets the breaker's crest head on or directly astern.

7-36. The breaker or wave period affects the speed at which the craft encounters breaking waves. Short period storm waves from local sources may occur every 6 to 12 seconds. At this frequency, a craft does not have the opportunity to pass the breaking wave. Such continuous impact may cause an operator to lose his bearing and become disoriented. Long period waves may occur every 10 to 20 seconds. On steep beaches, landing craft can pass through the breaker zone between waves.

7-37. Surf characteristics can vary considerably with respect to time and location. A sequence of waves often seems to have regular characteristics, but surf characteristics are as irregular as the ocean bottom topography over which the swell travels en route to the beach. Any wave system can develop an exceptionally high wave.

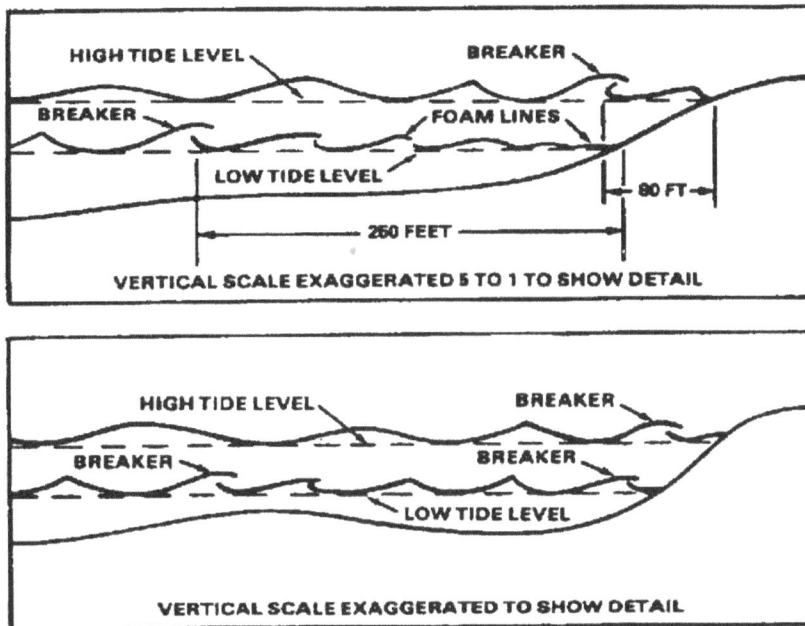

Figure 7-2. Effect of Tide on Surf Zone

7-38. The importance of beach slope to surf is in its effect on the width of the surf zone. The breaker line that represents the seaward border of the surf zone is found where the depth to the bottom is about 1.3 times the significant breaker height. With 6-foot breakers, the breaker line is located where the depth to the bottom is about 8 feet, regardless of slope. On a beach with a slope of 1:10, the breaker line for 6-foot breakers would be about 80 feet (24.4m) from the shoreline; with a slope of 1:50, about 400 feet (Figure 7-2). Off a very steep beach, there are no lines of foam inside the breaker line. After breaking, each wave rushes violently up the shore face and hits any beached craft with great force. On a flat beach, there are numerous lines of advancing foam. The energy of the waves is expended during the advance through the surf zone, and there is only a gentle up rush and backrush on the beach. Beaches with a slight gradient may require use of causeways to offload cargo.

7-39. The portion of a wave over a submarine ridge slows down, while the portion on either side swings in toward the ridge. When the waves swing together, each crest is squeezed and the wave height increases. Heavy surf is found wherever a submarine ridge runs out from a coast. A submarine canyon has the opposite effect. The portion of the wave over the canyon travels faster than the portions on either side, and then fans out. When the wave fans out, the crest is stretched and wave height decreases. The amount of protection afforded by headlands, peninsulas, islands, and other obstructions depends as much on underwater topography as on the coastline's shape.

TIDE

7-40. Planning for tide must be incorporated early in the planning stages of every water transport operation. Tide is the periodic rise and fall of water caused mainly by the gravitational effect of the moon and the sun on the rotating earth. In addition to the rise and fall in a vertical plane, there is horizontal movement called tidal current. When the tidal current flows shoreward, it is called flood current; when it flows seaward, it is ebb current. High tide, or high water, is the rising tide's maximum height. Low tide, or low water, is the falling tide's minimum height. The difference between the level of water at high and low tides is the range of tide.

7-41. The period of tide is the time interval from one low tide to the following low tide or from one high tide to the next high tide. These intervals average 12 hours and 25 minutes at most places. About every 2 weeks, during the new moon and the full moon, the highest high water and the lowest low water occur. The combined attractive influences of the sun and moon on the water at these times cause this unusually large range of tide. These tides are spring tides. When the moon is in its first and third quarters, the attractive influences of the sun and the moon oppose each other and the range of tide is unusually small. Tides during these times are neap tides. Tides occurring when the moon is at its maximum semimonthly decline are called tropic tides. During tropic tides, the daily range increases. Tidal range also varies with coastal configuration and barometric pressure.

7-42. The stage of the tide affects the width of the beach and, accordingly, the type of surf, the depth of water over sandbars and reefs, the width of exposed beach that must be traversed, and the requirements for special equipment to facilitate debarkation. Extreme tidal ranges may restrict unloading to the period of high tide. This requires maximum speed of operation and a rapid, heavy buildup of supplies in the early stages of a landing. If there is a relatively large tidal range on a gently sloping beach, water may rise or descend on the beach so rapidly that craft are stranded on a dry bottom before they can retract. This may put a critical number of craft out of action until the next rise of tide.

7-43. If, in addition to a flat gradient, the bottom has many irregularities, a fall in the tide may ground craft far from the beach proper. Personnel will have to debark and wade ashore through these pools. If the pools are deep, a considerable loss of equipment can be expected. In some cases the effect of the tide may require that craft be held at the beach as the tide recedes, discharging their cargo while resting high and dry on the exposed beach. The craft then retracts on the following tide.

7-44. The force of an unusually strong wind exerted on the tide at the landing area may greatly alter the width of beach available for operations. Along with an ebbing tide, a strong offshore wind may blow all the water off the beach and, on a gentle gradient, the water level may recede to an extreme distance from the beach proper. Personnel and material must then pass over a wide exposed beach. On the other hand, a powerful onshore wind can increase the advance of high tide to such an extent that beach installations and activities are endangered or flooded.

7-45. Where obstacles do not exist, a landing on a flood tide is generally preferred so that craft may be beached and retracted readily. Normally, it is desirable to set the time for landing 2 or 3 hours before high tide. It is not advised to load a craft when a high tide is going out and the depth close to the ship's draft. The result may be a loaded craft, unable to retract. References are kept on every vessel for predicting area tides, and the crew is trained to use these manuals.

WIND

7-46. Wind velocity, the distance spanned by the wind, the duration of the wind, and decay distance influence swell and surf functions on the beach. Winds at or near the surface of the earth have been classified, and their characteristics are known and predictable. Some surface winds are very deep and extend for miles into the air. Some are shallow, such as the land breeze, and extend only a few hundred feet (meters) above the surface. Winds aloft may blow in a direction opposite to surface winds. Velocity and direction may vary with different elevations. The velocity and duration of the wind and the size of the water area over which the wind has acted to produce waves, govern the growth of waves. Swells are waves that have progressed beyond the area of influence of the generating winds. A very rough sea disrupts landing schedules and formations by restricting the speed and maneuverability of craft. Normal control and coordination problems become more complex.

7-47. Planners must consider the effects of heavy seas on personnel and landing craft when establishing timetables, distances to be traveled on the water, and loads to be carried. With an excessive or poorly distributed load, vessels may list severely or even sink. Extremely rough conditions may necessitate removing loads from the craft and placing the craft aboard another vessel or in a safe haven. When a rough sea is anticipated, craft carry smaller loads and proceed cautiously. Ship-to-shore distances are reduced as much as feasible. Since the unloading of equipment and supplies may be restricted by heavy seas, priorities must be established for critical items so that the most essential shore requirements are met as quickly as possible.

WEATHER INFORMATION

7-48. Weather information about the area of operations must be analyzed carefully to determine the probable effect of weather on craft operations and working conditions. Early in the planning stage, the battalion commander must find out what source will furnish weather information and in what manner. The success of a tactical operation may depend on a sequence of several favorable days after the initial landing has been made. The most important consideration is the sea and swell caused by high winds and storms. Excessive sea and swell may end the movement of later serials, thus placing the assault troops in a precarious position ashore. Planners must consider beaching conditions, unloading conditions, speed of vessels, the effect of wind and sea on the tides, and the physical condition of the troops. Alternate plans for a water transport movement must consider possible variations from average weather.

7-49. Weather conditions en route to the area must also be considered. In a tactical operation, maximum advantage must be taken of weather conditions that might conceal an approach to the objective area. If the approach is made in calm, clear weather, the enemy can locate the attack force and the landing area more easily, and his air attacks will not be impeded. Bad weather, storms, fog, and winds affect the movement, but they also force the enemy to rely on more indirect and less dependable means of attack and of determining the target area. Weather information is a communications priority so that plans may be made or altered without delay, especially if unusual weather conditions are anticipated. In estimating the effects of weather on an operation, planners must consider the:

- Direction and speed of winds at the surface and in the upper air, the likelihood of storms, and the nature of storms typical to the target area.

- Distance at which objects can be seen horizontally at the surface and both horizontally and vertically in the upper air.

- Restrictions imposed on visibility by fog, haze, rain, sleet, or snow.

- Effect of extreme temperatures, excessive rain, snow or ice on personnel and materiel.

WEATHER FORECASTS

7-50. Weather prediction is based on an understanding of weather processes and observations of present conditions. Weather forecasts are based on past changes and present trends. In areas supported by weather radar and where weather patterns follow with great regularity, the probability of an accurate forecast is very high. In transitional areas (or areas where an inadequate number of reports is available), the forecasts are less reliable. Such forecasts are based on principles of probability, and high reliability should not be expected. Long-term forecasts for two (2) weeks or a month in advance are limited to general statements.

7-51. Synoptic forecasts are used mainly for day-to-day forecasts. They are developed from reports received from a widespread network of stations that make simultaneous observations at prescribed times. Data from these observations are transmitted to a weather center and analyzed. The resulting forecast is forwarded to the operating units concerned. This type of forecast requires a dependable system of communications. The observers must be located over a wide area, possibly including enemy territory. Synoptic forecasts suitable for landing operations can be made only 1 to 2 days before the operation, but such forecasts will generally be dependable.

7-52. A Harbormaster Command & Control Center (HCCC) has equipment enabling it to gather immediate weather data, pertinent to landing forces, and deliver it to lighters approaching the AO.

7-53. Conditions beyond the range of synoptic forecasts are estimated by the statistical method. This method relies on weather observations accumulated over a period of years and describes the average weather that may be expected in a given area. It shows such information as the strength and direction of prevailing winds, average temperatures, and average precipitation. If weather records at a given area have been kept for a number of years, the statistical study will be correct about 65 percent of the time.

7-54. The services of a trained meteorologist should be used whenever possible.

7-55. Data about average weather conditions are essential in planning a landing operation, but assault landings require current information. A forecast that is 24 to 36 hours old is not reliable. Marine forecasts are available via satellite over internet sites for those vessels with satellite communications capability, including INMARSAT.

7-56. Weather forecasts are passed to vessels and affected units via data, fax, or voice. Wind and sea state forecasts over water are given in the Beaufort Scale (Table 7-1), which is used by most weather forecasters. Sea State is taken from the Force column.

7-57. The Modified Surf Index (MSI) is obtained from weather forecasters, and applied using the Watercraft Risk Impact Rules (Table 7-2). The MSI is a calculated, single dimensionless number used as an objective decision aid. It is an assessment of the combined effects of breakers, littoral current, and wind conditions on landing craft. If the MSI exceeds the MSI limit for a particular craft, the landing is not feasible with that type of craft without increasing the casualty rate.

7-58. To apply the Watercraft Risk Impact Rules to an operation, the leader inserts the available current or forecasted weather information within the outlined weather parameters. The leader may cease some or all operations for affected watercraft, according to the table. Category 1 watercraft are most susceptible to risk in adverse weather conditions and will usually be first to index in an operation.

Table 7-1. Beaufort scale

The Beaufort Scale: <u>Sea State Specification</u>

Force	Speed		Description	Specifications
	MPH	knots		
0	0-1	0-1	Calm	Sea like a mirror
1	1-3	1-3	Light air	Ripple with the appearance of scales are formed, but without foam crests.
2	4-7	4-6	Light Breeze	Small wavelets, still short, but more pronounced. Crests have a glassy appearance and do not break.
3	8-12	7-10	Gentle Breeze	Large wavelets. Crests begin to break. Foam of glassy appearance. Perhaps scattered white horses.
4	13-18	11-16	Moderate Breeze	Small waves, becoming larger; frequent white horses.
5	19-24	17-21	Fresh Breeze	Moderate waves, taking a more pronounced long form; many white horses are formed. Chance of some spray.
6	25-31	22-27	Strong Breeze	Large waves begin to form; the white foam crests are more extensive everywhere. Probably some spray.
7	32-38	28-33	Near Gale	Sea heaps up and white foam from breaking waves blown in streaks along the direction of the wind.
8	39-46	34-40	Gale	Moderately high waves of greater length; edges of crests begin to break into spindrift. The foam is blown in well-marked streaks along the direction of the wind.
9	47-54	41-47	Severe Gale	High waves. Dense streaks of foam along the direction of the wind. Crests of waves begin to topple, tumble and roll over. Spray may affect visibility.
10	55-63	48-55	Storm	Very high waves with long overhanging crests. The resulting foam, in great patches, is blown in dense white streaks along the direction of the wind. On the whole the surface of the sea takes on a white appearance. The 'tumbling' of the sea becomes heavy and shock-like. Visibility affected.
11	64-72	56-63	Violent Storm	Exceptionally high waves (small ships might be lost to view behind the waves). The sea is completely covered with long white patches of foam lying along the direction of the wind. Everywhere the edges of the wave crests are blown into froth. Visibility affected.
12	73-83	64-71	Hurricane	The air is filled with foam and spray. Sea completely white with driving spray; visibility seriously affected.

The Beaufort Scale of Wind Force runs from force 0 (calm) to force 12 (Hurricane). The Meteorological Offices issue Gale Warnings for sea areas when wind force 8 or greater is forecast.

SHIPSIDE PROCEDURE

7-59. Loading cargo into a lighter from a vessel anchored in the stream is difficult and somewhat dangerous. The shipboard control point, typically operated by a cell from the Terminal Battalion Harbormaster, must consider the conditions under which the ship is being unloaded. They must constantly coordinate with the lighter crews at shipside to ensure safety precautions are being followed. If it is determined that continuing the discharge operation is dangerous, they must immediately notify the ship's captain, the lighter control center, and the various unit commanders supporting the operation. The terminal commander or vessel master will decide whether to continue operations or suspend them until conditions improve.

7-60. The following variables influence the ship discharge rate:

- Cargo type to be unloaded (mobile, containerized, unitized, or loose) and characteristics of the cargo ship.
- Material Handling Equipment (MHE) available and experience of the cargo handling personnel on the ship and ashore.
- Environmental factors such as weather conditions, beach characteristics and distance cargo ships are from the beach.
- Enemy threats.

7-61. Unless unusual wind or tidal currents exist, the ship normally anchors bow to either the wind or current, whichever is stronger. If all hatches are being worked, lighters may receive cargo over both sides of the ship or at the stern. For example, the cargo from Hold 1 may be discharged over the starboard side and cargo from Hold 2 over the port side.

7-62. If sea and weather conditions prevent cargo discharge from both sides of a ship at anchor, the method of discharge must be changed. The vessel must be moored both bow and stern to avoid swinging to the tide or wind. The lighters should come along the lee side of the vessel and be moored to the vessel to receive cargo. This operation reduces the discharge rate about 50%. Beach control personnel or the shipboard control point NCO direct lighter operators to the number of the hatch and the side of the ship where they should moor. Detailed procedures for coming alongside, mooring, and clearing shipside are in FM 55-501. Drafts of non-unitized small items of cargo are usually handled in cargo nets, which are unhooked and left in the craft. Empty nets are returned to the ship each time the lighter comes alongside for another load.

Table 7-2. Watercraft Risk Impact Rules

Leadership must recognize weather conditions that impact water transport operations. Receipt of regular weather forecasts and application of the forecasts to operations may be conducted using the Watercraft Risk Impact Rules (Table 5-2). **Category**	Yellow	Red
Cat 1 Watercraft Floating Causeway, RRDF, SLWT, Causeway Ferry	Sea State >= 2 MSI >= 5 Visibility < 1 mile Freezing drizzle Winds > 30 kts	Sea State >= 3 MSI >= 6 Visibility < 1/2 mile Freezing rain Winds > 50 kts
Cat 2 Watercraft LCM, JHSV, 65' Tug, 100' Tug	Sea State >= 2.5 MSI >= 7 Visibility < 1 mile Freezing drizzle Winds > 30 kts	Sea State >= 3.5 MSI >= 8 Visibility < 1/2 mile Freezing rain Winds > 50 kts
Cat 3 Watercraft LCU 2000, LSV, 128' Tug	Sea State >= 3 MSI >= 10 Visibility < 1 mile Freezing drizzle Winds > 30 kts	Sea State >= 4 MSI >= 12 Visibility < 1/2 mile Freezing rain Winds > 50 kts

SALVAGE OPERATIONS

7-63. The main objective of salvage operations during LOTS is to keep the beach and sea approaches clear. Experienced salvage personnel never lose sight of this mission. Even when freeing a single stranded or disabled craft, they do not impede beach or offshore operations.

7-64. To keep the beach clear, craft that can be repaired or removed quickly are given priority. Vessels that cannot be salvaged readily are anchored securely and left at the beach until traffic eases and more time can be devoted to them. Salvage crews must act quickly when a landing craft broaches to the shore and is stranded. Speedy assistance often prevents serious damage to vessels, especially in heavy surf. Fast recovery from seaward is usually the best procedure for salvaging broached-to vessels. Methods of recovery are listed in FM 55-501.

7-65. When a loaded craft is aground offshore, any practical system to expedite the unloading of cargo from the craft should be used. Cargo in small, packaged containers up to 40 pounds can be handed over the side. Cargo boxes placed at the rail of the craft may serve as steps and facilitate cargo handling.

7-66. Rough-terrain cranes may lift cargo too heavy to be moved by hand. The Barge Derrick crane is moved to the location of the stranded craft if intervening depth and surf conditions permit. A bulldozer may push stranded craft back into the water. The blade of the bulldozer must be padded by fenders, salvaged tires, or similar material to prevent damage to the hulls or ramps of the craft. To maximize salvage capability, one bulldozer should be readily available to each operational beach.

7-67. No craft is ever left on the beach unattended or unwatched. The operator must remain constantly at the controls while beaching, loading, unloading, and retracting.

ANTIBROACHING MEASURES

7-68. The best insurance against broaching to is an alert, skilled operator who knows the capabilities and limitations of his craft. Normally, anti-broaching aids are not used if the craft is to be unloaded quickly and retracted from the beach immediately. Under most conditions, anti-broaching lines from the bow or stern of the beached craft are impractical. Anti-broaching anchors or lines may be used in extreme surf conditions, where a crosscurrent may cause broaching. However, the operator must keep in mind that this method is time-consuming, severely restricts the number of craft that can be off-loaded along a specific sector of the beach, and is often ineffective in preventing broaching.

7-69. The master of a landing craft keeps the craft in position on the beach by properly using engines, rudders, and stern anchors. (The LCM-8 is not equipped with a stern anchor.) If the LCU and LCM-8 are beaching on the same sector of beach, the LCM-8 is somewhat protected if it is beached leeward of the LCU. For example, if three LCUs are on the same beach, one or two LCM-8s can be beached and discharged in the partially protected zone on the lee side of each LCU. When the LCM-8 and LCU are loaded with similar cargo, two or more LCM-8s can usually be unloaded in the time required to discharge an LCU. Preventive and recovery procedures for broached craft are in FM 55-501.

SUMMARY

7-70. Logistics over the Shore (LOTS) provides the joint commander ability to maneuver combat power and sustainment to and across bare beach environments. The ability to circumvent obstacles that prevent military use of strategic ports, and maneuver combat power at-will is at the heart of the mission of Army watercraft. The tailorable nature of LOTS and variety of organic watercraft available within the Army to perform this vital task is essential to closing and sustaining the force to meet the Army mission.

Chapter 8

Terminal Support Operations

TYPES OF SUPPORT CRAFT

8-1.   Several types of watercraft can be used to support terminal operations. They include high speed vessels, landing craft, tugs, self propelled and towed commercial and military cranes and barges, and causeway systems. Logisticians must be prepared to work with whatever assets are available.

WATER TRANSPORT LINES OF COMMUNICATION (LOC)

8-2.   When required, water transport lines of communication are formed to control and operate a waterway system at a terminal; to formulate and coordinate plans for using resources at the port and along the littorals; and to integrate and supervise local civilian facilities used to support military operations.

ORGANIZING A WATER TRANSPORT LOC

8-3.   Three separate functional components make up a water transport LOC system: the Ocean Reception Point (ORP), the littoral waterway, and the water terminal. The ocean reception point consists of mooring points for ships, a marshaling area for barges, and a control point. The mooring point can be alongside a wharf, at an inland anchorage or anchored offshore. The marshaling areas can be alongside a wharf or secured to stake barges at anchor. The control point can be ashore or on a stake barge. Stake barges at the ORP can be semi permanent anchored barges or vessels. Barges can be used to house control point crews as well as the small tug crews, dispatchers, and other personnel connected with the ORP. The ORP stake barges should have gear lockers to stow the various equipment and lines needed to service barges and tugs. There should be at least two stake barges at the ORP; one for import and one for export.

8-4.   The US Army Corps of Engineers operates and maintains the inland waterway in a generic theater or in CONUS. However, the host country normally maintains and operates developed inland waterway systems in overseas theaters. Aids to navigation on the inland waterways differ all over the world. Some areas do not use aids, while others use the international ocean system. The U.S. uses many different and highly sophisticated systems. For illustrations of navigation aids, and the types used worldwide, refer to FM 55-501. The inland water terminal is where cargo is transferred between a ship or vessel and land-based transportation. Terminals vary in size and design; some are designed for one commodity, others, for general purposes. For military purposes, the available terminal may not be what is needed; therefore, the planner and user must adapt (at least until engineers can modify the terminal). Quays running along the river front, finger piers at wider points, or basin type terminals could be adapted by installing quays or piers, installing regular barges by either partially sinking or driving pilings to hold them in place, or using a beach that could be improved.

LOGISTICS PLANNING

8-5.   The logistician's interest in an inland waterway is in its capability to move cargo. Therefore, he is interested in the effect of its physical features on its ability to carry cargo. Among the physical features are the width and depth of channel; horizontal and vertical clearance of bridges; number of locks, their method of operations, and length of time required for craft to clear them. Freeze-ups, floods, and droughts also affect a waterway's capacity. The transportation planner must anticipate these seasonal restrictions. The planner must also be aware of the speed, fluctuation, and direction of water current as well as availability of craft, labor, terminal facilities, and maintenance support available.

8-6.   Waterway capacity is based on turnaround time -the period between leaving a point and returning to it. Since barges are being picked up at a wharf or stake barge, barge loading time is not part of the computation. If barges are picked up at shipside without marshaling at a wharf or stake barge, loading time of the barge would become a factor of turnaround time. Craft loading and unloading times must be taken into account.

PLANNING CONSIDERATIONS

8-7.   Length of haul is the trip distance between the barge pickup point and unloading points or the reverse trip.

8-8.   Speed is influenced by wind, current, power of craft, and size of load. If the craft's speed cannot be determined, assume it is 5 nautical miles per hour (knots) in still water (9.3 kilometers per hour). Speed and direction of current can frequently be discounted since resistance in one direction may be balanced by assistance in the other direction. However, this is not always the case.

8-9.   Speed control is required because of possible damage by the vessel's wake to the inland waterway, loading and unloading time is the time to load and unload a craft at origin and destination.

8-10.   Time consumed in locks is the time it takes a craft and its tow to pass through a lock. When exact data is lacking, assume lock time is one hour per single lock.

8-11.   Hours of operations are usually planned as 24 hours per day. Maintenance factors are applied in equipment requirements as shown later in formulas.

8-12.   Transit time is the time to move the craft the length of the haul and directly related occurrences. To determine transit time, add the time to make up the tow, the distance divided by the speed of the tow; the time consumed to pass through the locks; and the time to break up the tow.

8-13.   When determining the number of barges, tugboats, or craft requirements, always roundup to the nearest whole number. Then apply the maintenance factor and round up again.

8-14.   Two basic types of inland waterway watercraft systems using barges are: barge-carrying ships and ships' cargo discharged onto barges at the ORP.

8-15.   Ship schedules furnish the barges used on the inland waterway system.

TOWING OPERATIONS

8-16.   Towing is a well-developed maritime procedure. Rescue and salvage towing generates a necessary sense of urgency. Conditions of a tow, weather, war zones, and other factors commonly make towing a time-critical operation. While certain ships and watercraft are designed to offer towing services, all ships can take a tow in an emergency. Towing is a routine operation for tugs. Good practice of seamanship is necessary to accomplish the mission without endangering the tow, tug, personnel, or operational schedules. While many trans-oceanic and coastal tows are completed uneventfully, the crew must be prepared to handle emergency conditions. Good planning, preparation for emergency situations, and correct ship handling are necessary elements of towing.

Tow Planning Factors

8-17.   Present day towing has evolved throughout the history of engine-powered towing. There are distinct differences between simple barge towing, open water coastal and ocean towing.

8-18. Schedule harbor tug support so ocean-towing tugs are not kept waiting unnecessarily for passing of tows at the Ocean Reception Point (ORP).

8-19. When the draft of the ocean-towing tugs is too great for the depth of water at either terminal, prearrange the delivery or take-over of the tow before the ocean tug arrives at the ORP.

8-20. Estimate the required towline pull and horsepower of the towing vessel before assigning a tug for a mission. Use the correct size of tug for the job.

8-21. Use the proper craft for the job. While all vessels are capable of towing for a short time in an emergency, only tugs are designed to do so. Do not use unsuitable craft to do work beyond their capacity (consider the towline pull). For instance, do not use a landing craft to tow another landing craft over great distances.

8-22. If another vessel can conduct the mission, do not use a tug unnecessarily. For instance, use an LCM to move small numbers of people between shore and ship.

8-23. Ensure tugs have proper endurance (range and capacity) for the mission. Arrange provisioning or refueling en route if necessary.

8-24. Ensure tugs in forward areas have sufficient stability, reserve buoyancy, and protection from small arms attacks.

8-25. Do not use tugs unnecessarily for standby duty on salvage or rescue operations. Tugs should not be ordered to stand by unless there is a definite possibility that their services may be needed and they can render the service likely to be required.

8-26. Do not remove tugs unnecessarily from areas where tugs equipped for rescue (salvage or firefighting) may be required.

TYPES OF TOWING MISSIONS

There are two general types of towing missions.

8-27. **Administrative towing missions** are routine in nature. Tugs reposition floating equipment within the confines of the terminal harbor areas; dock, undock, and assist large ships in port arrivals/departures; and perform short range missions in protected waters where only light towing gear and equipment is required. Administrative towing usually requires towing gear and equipment normally found aboard as part of the tug's basic issue items. These items are wire rope bridles and pendants, shackles, wire rope clips, and swivels. This equipment is well suited for short duration towing in waters protected from the effects of coastal and ocean seas.

Special towing missions generally transit unprotected coastal waters and the open ocean. These missions require considerably larger and stronger tugs using heavier and stronger towing gear to withstand the violent stresses encountered in open coastal and ocean seas. Normally, these tugs have greater towing power (larger engines and overall heavier equipment and construction) and are equipped with towing machinery, such as single- and double-drum wire rope towing winches; tow wire guides, rollers, and pinions; cranes or winch/boom assemblies to handle the tow rigging; and a small workboat for boarding and inspecting the tow while enroute.

Towing gear for these missions include heavy chain bridles and pendants (anchor chain), plate shackles, retrieving wires, emergency towing bridles, towlines (hawsers), flooding alarms, pumps, and anchors. Large floating equipment, such as floating cranes (BD), is equipped with their own towing gear. Such heavy gear cannot be carried as basic issue items aboard tugs because of weight and cube.

8-28. Rescue/salvage towing missions have two forms: planned and opportunistic. Planned rescue and salvage towing requires generally the same conditions of a special towing mission, with some additional considerations. An additional hazard is trying to tow equipment that is not seaworthy because of battle damage, grounding or other non-operational status. Opportunistic rescue and salvage towing occurs when any ship or tug is in the immediate area of a vessel requiring towing assistance to remove it from immediate danger. This type of towing uses any means at hand to remove the stricken vessel from danger. The nature of the operation makes it extremely hazardous to the towing vessel as well as the towed vessel.

TOWING RESPONSIBILITIES

8-29. The command requesting tow of craft must provide the craft in seaworthy condition with flooding alarms, navigation lights, electrical power for alarms and lights, salvage gear (anchors and pumps), and towing gear (bridle, pendant, and retrieving wires). For suspect or deficient seaworthiness conditions, both the tow and towing command must agree on the risk of tow. The command accepting the tow mission must provide tug and towing gear to connect to the towed craft's towing gear. The tug and gear must be seaworthy for the particular mission route and have the appropriate size, horsepower, and control to safely and successfully accomplish the towing mission. On accepting the tow, the towing command accepts full responsibility. Before accepting, seaworthiness must be verified. The tow should be refused if it is considered not fit for sea. Towing is accepted only after the tug's officers complete a comprehensive evaluation and survey of the tow.

SEAWORTHINESS

8-30. Towing seaworthiness means suitable condition for the mission. This concerns all the various technical implications of the tow and towing vessel.

8-31. When insuring seaworthiness of the tow and towing vessel, consider the following: Vessel design and specifications, Structural condition and stability, Age, maintenance history, and status, Reinforcement requirements, and Hull and superstructure closures.

8-32. The towing gear is very important to the success of the tow. Inspect and insure the adequacy of towing gear, including the following: Dewatering facilities, Chafing gear, Firefighting and damage control facilities, emergency towing gear.

8-33. Additional considerations include repair parts to be carried, tow-boarding facilities, waters to be transited, and hazards of the route.

8-34. A certificate of seaworthiness for ocean tows must be completed. The certificate indicates the general characteristics of the tow, type of cargo, towing gear, lights, and emergency gear aboard the tow. Hulls not considered seaworthy for open-ocean should be transported as deck cargo on heavy-lift, SEABEE, or float-on/float-off ships. Only under extreme emergency situations should open-ocean towing be attempted when the tow is not considered seaworthy, as there is an extremely high risk of sinking the towing vessel.

TOWING SHIPS

8-35. All ships can tow in an emergency; however, only properly designed and outfitted tugs make good towing ships. Characteristically, a tug's superstructure is set forward, allowing the towing point to be close to the ship's pivot point. The towing point is located far from the rudder and screws so that it allows the towline to sweep the stern rail. High horsepower, slow speed, large rudder, towing machine, power capstans, towing points, and a clear fantail characterize a good tug. All ships can tow and be towed in an emergency. Ships not equipped for towing can use the anchor chain, wire straps, nylon lines, or any combination necessary. A good catenary ensures spring in the towline. Slow speed transfers the lowest dynamic load from the towing ship to the tow. Large ships can easily overpower the tow and excessively strain the towline. The towing ship should keep engine revolutions low for the highest torque and lowest strain and surging.

ROUTINE AND RESCUE TOWING

8-36. Administrative point-to-point towing is routine and ensures that both the tug and tow are seaworthy and prepared for the transit. Rescue towing requires prompt action, often under pressing circumstances of a war zone, salvage operation, or inclement weather.

MANNED TOWS

8-37. If a continuous watch is required on the tow, a riding crew is placed aboard the tow. The riding crew provides security, fire watch, damage control, line handling, communication, flooding watch, and defense. It provides the nucleus for fire fighting, damage control, and defensive actions. Under normal conditions, and after proper securing for sea, most tows can be done without a riding crew. However, there are exceptions. It is far better to secure the tow properly than to provide a riding crew as a substitute security.

UNMANNED TOWS

8-38. Barges, floating cranes, dredges, pontoons, pile drivers, dry docks, and ships can be towed without riding crews. Any hull considered seaworthy can be towed unmanned.

8-39. A seaworthy hull has watertight integrity, structural soundness, proper position of the centers of gravity and buoyancy, and good stability characteristics.

8-40. All cargo and equipment is secured. Long-distance and valuable tows without a riding crew should be periodically boarded and inspected. Since the operation is often difficult and hampered by weather and sea condition, the inspection should be well planned and executed promptly and efficiently. Using an inflatable boat to transport the inspecting party to and from the tow is recommended. This boat should be equipped with an outboard engine whether or not it is veered aft on a line. This greatly enhances its maneuverability and permits its recovery if the veering line parts.

8-41. When preparing a crane, dredge, pile driver, or other floating equipment designed for operation in sheltered waters, it may be necessary to remove high weights; to secure booms, ladders, deck structures, ballast, and trim; and to perform other unique functions due to the hull's design.

8-42. Senior marine deck and engineering officers (MOS 880A2/881A2) with tow preparation experience should thoroughly analyze the configuration and modifications to the hull and recommend it for open-ocean towing. Nothing is derived from taking a marginal tow to sea only to lose it.

INSPECTION OF TOWS

8-43. Towing can be a dangerous operation. Inspections must be complete and comprehensive. The following is a list of items to be considered when planning a tow.

8-44. Tows should be properly trimmed, not overloaded, and secured for sea.

8-45. Deficiencies must be identified and corrected before acceptance.

8-46. Inspect all secured gear to ensure it is properly tied down. Turnbuckles with wire rope tie-downs with good holding results should be used. Manila line lashings effectively hold light gear. After all gear is secured, tie-downs and lashings are inspected to ensure all are taut and holding. Retightening of turnbuckles and lashings may be necessary during long-range tows or prolonged periods of time. This requires the tug's crew to board the tow at sea, an inherently dangerous task.

8-47. When large units of high weight must be secured for sea, it is advantageous to weld them to the deck. Welding requires extra time and effort – plan for it.

8-48. Tows are generally not dry-docked for inspection before being accepted. Suitable hull inspection consists of divers and internal observation and measurements. If a number of checks along the sides, between light and full load waterlines show adequate thickness of the original hull side plating, the bottom of the craft to be towed can be assumed to be sound.

8-49. A thorough internal inspection should be made. Note the bottom framing, plating, and welds in the forward one-fifth of the craft's overall length. If no evidence of serious deterioration or displacement of hull plating exists, the craft can be considered structurally sound. If the inspection uncovers serious rusting or displacement of the frames, plating, bottom, or weld seams (particularly in the forward one-fifth of the craft's length), the craft should be dry-docked and necessary repairs made. While in dry dock, magnetic particle checks (or their equivalent) of bottom, side, butts, joints, decks, and inner bottom should be made. All defective welds and plating should be repaired or replaced. Structural reinforcing and load distribution may be accomplished with wood timbers. Craft should be examined thoroughly before towing to avoid special dry-docking of craft. Thickness and magnetic particle checks made during cyclic maintenance and resulting repairs should provide suitable supporting data to avoid special dry-docking. All flooding alarm systems should be inspected for proper installation and operations.

8-50. Navigational lights should be tested.

8-51. Batteries, including hydrometer reading, should be inspected and tested. There must be sufficient battery capacity to support the systems for the duration of the mission.

8-52. All flooding alarms and navigation lights should have automatic lamp changers.

8-53. Packing glands in the stern tube should be checked. The shafts should be properly locked. If a riding crew is aboard, shafts may be allowed to freewheel.

8-54. The craft's rudder must be locked amidships to prevent erratic behavior of the tow.

TOWING RISK FACTORS

8-55. Commanding officers of the towing ship and the towed craft should agree to the conditions of risk in towing the craft. Risk conditions are based on the seaworthiness and structural condition of the tow, expected sea and weather conditions for the route, and the specifications of the towing ship. In acceptable risk, the hull, equipment, towing gear, and towing ship are seaworthy and structurally sound. In calculated risk, tow deficiencies are accepted but mitigated. The probability of tow safely reaching destination varies with deficiencies. A detailed risk assessment shall be conducted for all tows.

CHAIN OF COMMAND FOR TOWING/TOWED VESSEL

8-56. The commanding officer of the towing ship administers the tow, even when the tow has a riding crew with an officer in charge. In assuming this responsibility, the commanding officer of the towing ship inspects administrative conditions on the tow, with particular attention to personnel accounting, sanitation facilities, safety, security, and lifesaving equipment on board, general stores, provisions, equipment, and gear, communications, and defensive capability.

8-57. If the tow is not satisfactorily prepared, the commanding officer of the towing ship will so inform the tow's command to correct deficiencies.

AMPHIBIOUS OPERATIONS

8-58. The Army has used watercraft to land men and materiel since the Revolutionary War. The US Navy and Marines amphibious capability is a small package designed with limited sustainment to gain a foothold or conduct limited operations in the beginning of a deployment, or may not be available to support land-based operations. The Army has historically conducted large scale and sustained amphibious operations, and continues to do so.

8-59. There are four types of amphibious operations:

- Amphibious assault - involves landing and establishing forces on a hostile shore.

- Amphibious withdrawal - forces depart a hostile shore in naval ships or craft.

- Amphibious demonstration is designed to deceive the enemy by a show of force that deludes him into an unfavorable action.

- Amphibious raid - forces land from the sea on a hostile shore intending to occupy it only temporarily, with the objective to inflict loss or damage, secure information, create a diversion, or evacuate individuals and materiel.

8-60. The phases of an amphibious operation follow a well-defined pattern or sequence of events or activities – some overlap. This chapter discusses the activities in the general sequence of planning, embarkation, rehearsal, movement to the objective area, and assault and capture of the objective area. This chapter also provides watercraft commanders and operators the basic guidance Army water transport units need to participate in amphibious operations that support an Army or joint force.

PLANNING PHASE

8-61. Planning is the period between the issuance of the initiating directive to embarkation. It is a continuous process that extends from the time the initiating directive is issued to the end of the operation. Normally, Navy and Marine assault units conduct amphibious combat operations. It is at this point that the Army must identify the potential site where characteristics for a LOTS operation can be met, and this area is identified to the amphibious assault command so that it is secured early in the amphibious assault phase. Army vessels are used as floating platforms for on-call supply movement and for general unloading after the beachhead has been secured. However, Army landing craft can be part of the assault force, such as occurred in Panama during Operation Just Cause. Planning for coordinated training with shore party elements and for operational employment begins when the initiating directive assigning a water transport unit to the joint amphibious task force is received. Immediate liaison is established between the water transport unit and the naval beach group to which it is attached. The shore party's mission is twofold: to clear the beaches so the assault elements can land and move across them, and to provide combat support and interim combat service support for the assault elements.

8-62. Plans must be flexible so that combat demands can be met. The need to coordinate the detailed actions of all forces involved complicates planning for an amphibious operation. Consequently, planning must be concurrent, parallel, and detailed. In addition to a primary plan, alternate plans must be developed. During the planning phase, training shortfalls need to be corrected. As plans are developed, appropriate personnel must be briefed on the overall concept and their individual and collective responsibilities.

EMBARKATION PHASE

8-63. During the embarkation phase, the landing forces assigned to the amphibious task force, with their equipment and supplies, are assembled and loaded in assigned shipping sequence. This sequence is designed to support the landing plan and the scheme of maneuver ashore. Before the assault shipping arrives, water transport unit commanders, troop commanders, naval commanders, and shore party commanders prepare detailed embarkation and landing plans.

8-64. Large lighters can self-deploy or smaller lighters can be moved to the amphibious objective area aboard landing ships or assault ships. The type and numbers of lighters that each ship carries are identified by hull number.

8-65. The senior water transport unit representative on each ship, the commanding officer of troops, and the ship's officer in charge of cargo operations arrange the following:

- Billet assignments.
- Assignment of crews, relief crews, and maintenance teams.
- Assignment of working parties.
- Storage for fuel, lubricants, and maintenance material. Items must be available en route and during initial stages of the assault.
- Security details.
- Messing procedures.
- Stowage of weapons and ammunition.

8-66. Supplies and equipment must be prepared for loading before the assault shipping arrives. Lighters should be completely serviced, fuel and water cans filled, accessories placed, and radio and navigation equipment waterproofed. A final inspection ensures all craft and equipment are ready for the operation. If ships are to be loaded offshore, the embarkation area should be organized so that amphibians use different beach areas (see LOTS Chapter). Lighters to be embarked aboard the same ship are marshaled together and escorted by guide vessels to their assigned craft. Craft are loaded aboard assault shipping so that debarkation in the amphibious objective area is in the proper order.

REHEARSAL PHASE

8-67. The rehearsal phase of is the period where elements the task force conduct one or more exercises under conditions similar to those expected at the beachhead. The purpose of the rehearsal is to test the adequacy of plans and communications, the timing of detailed operations, and the combat readiness of participating forces.

8-68. The three types of exercises are:

- Separate force rehearsals. Elements (e.g., advance and demonstration forces) whose tasks are not closely associated with those of the main body of the amphibious task force normally conduct separate rehearsals.
- Staff rehearsals. Conducted before integrated rehearsals, they usually take the form of command post or game board exercises. If possible, these exercises test communications facilities.
- Integrated rehearsals. The rehearsal phase should include at least two integrated rehearsals for the assault phase. The first rehearsal omits actual bombardment and unloading supplies but stresses communications and control in executing ship-to-shore movement. The final rehearsal, using the actual operations plan, includes actual combat conditions to the degree practical.

MOVEMENT PHASE

8-69. The fourth phase is the movement to the amphibious area. This includes the departure of ships from loading points, the passage at sea, and the approach to and arrival in assigned positions in the objective area. The task force is divided into movement groups which proceed on prescribed routes. Alternate routes are designated for emergency use. Movement groups are organized based on the speed of the ships involved and the time they are needed in the objective area.

8-70. Movement groups that arrive before D-day are the advance force. If surprise is essential, such a force may not be used or may move in just before the main body. The advance force prepares the objective area for assault. It conducts reconnaissance, minesweeping, preliminary bombardment, underwater demolitions, and air operations.

8-71. Movement groups arriving on D-day are the main body of the task force. They consist of one or more transport groups, landing ship groups, support groups, or carrier groups. Movement groups that arrive after D-day provide resupply after the initial assault. These massive operations involve moving materiel and personnel into the theater of operations to sustain the combat effort.

ASSAULT PHASE

8-72. The assault phase begins when the assault elements of the main body arrive at their assigned position in the objective area.

8-73. The assault phase includes a sequence of six activities or operations 1) The assault area is subjected to indirect fire and air bombardment, 2) Helicopters, landing ships and crafts, and amphibians move the landing force, 3) Assault elements of the landing force land in drop and landing zones and on the beaches, 4) Water transport, helicopter-borne, air-dropped, and air-landed forces unite and seize the beachhead, 5) Naval forces provide logistic, air, and naval gunfire support throughout the assault, and 6) Remaining landing force elements go ashore to conduct any operations required to support the mission.

8-74. The organization of landing ships, landing craft, and amphibious vehicles employed in assault landings parallels the landing force organization. The landing force is organized into a landing team. Landing teams consist of an infantry battalion or similar level combat unit reinforced with combat support and combat service support units. The teams, normally water transport or helicopter-borne, are organized into waves that contain troops and equipment that land at the same time. Vessel groups are the naval force's basic task organization for controlling amphibian vehicles and landing craft afloat. One vessel group is organized for each battalion landing team or its equivalent. The vessel group lands in the first wave of landing craft or amphibians. Vessel waves are the landing craft or amphibians within a vessel group that carry troops to be landed at the same time. Organizing into waves helps control the vessel group; command is through wave commanders rather than directly with individual vessel commanders. Vessel waves operate as a unit.

8-75. Ship-to-shore movement begins when ordered by the amphibious task force commander and ends when the unloading is complete. It may be divided into two periods: the assault and initial unloading period, and the general unloading period. The first period is tactical, and the second period is logistical. For ship-to-shore movement, tactical units are divided into special groupings and landed in successive waves. These waves are designated as scheduled, on-call, or nonscheduled units. Following the tactical units, supplies are landed at the discretion of the appropriate troop commander or as required by the landing force. Supplies so landed are designated as floating dumps or landing force supplies.

8-76. Scheduled waves normally consist of elements of the assault landing team, although other units may be included. The time and place for them to land are predetermined. On-call waves are also needed in the initial assault, but they have no fixed time and place for landing. On-call vessel waves are held in readiness in landing craft, ships, or amphibious vehicles near the primary assistant central control or approach lane control ships. On-call waves are landed when the landing force commander calls for them. Nonscheduled units are directed to land when the need for them ashore can be predicted with reasonable accuracy. They are held in readiness for landing during the initial unloading period but are not included in either scheduled or on-call waves. Floating dumps are preloaded in landing craft, landing ships, or amphibian vehicles to meet anticipated supply requirements. They remain near the line of departure and land when requested by the appropriate troop commander.

8-77. Army watercraft may land with the initial assault waves, but this is not normal practice. They usually serve as assault platforms, on-call elements or to deliver landing force supplies. Following landing of the initial waves, Army watercraft are stationed at designated control points until dispatched ashore by the lighter control officer. When dispatched ashore, the craft move to the designated beach for unloading. After unloading, they move to assigned assembly areas until routed to a specific ship for reloading. Army vessels continue to function in this manner throughout ship-to-shore movement until released by the shore party commander. Then they revert to the control of the at-sea commander or their parent organization.

8-78. In amphibious operations, the commander of the amphibious task force via the naval control officer exercises control of ship-to-shore movement. The shore party via attached naval beach parties carries out near-beach movement control. Water transport unit commanders remain water transport until the general unloading period begins. Then they move ashore with their control elements to coordinate with the shore party commander and the staff of the terminal battalion being phased ashore. When ashore, commanders establish company command posts and set up shore-based control systems. While waterborne, water transport commanders help the Harbormaster Detachment or maritime force control office dispatch and route craft and coordinate maintenance and supply activities for their units.

8-79. The assault phase ends when the task force mission is accomplished. When the assault phase ends, the amphibious operation ends, the amphibious task force is dissolved as an organization, and its elements are reassigned. Responsibility for further operations in the former amphibious objective area is transferred.

BEACH MARKERS

8-80. A system of beach markers is used while organizing the beach to receive landing craft, landing ships, and amphibians. The markers help vessel operators locate the correct beach in daylight or darkness. Shore party or Harbormaster Detachment personnel install the markers as soon as possible after the initial assault of an amphibious operation. Beaches under attack are color designated, such as red beach or green beach, with markers of corresponding colors. The daylight markers are made of cloth and held aloft. During daylight, a horizontal rectangle identifies the left flank of a beach, as seen from the sea; a square, the center of the beach; and a vertical cloth rectangle, the right flank. During night operations, a system of white and appropriately colored lights is used. When the tactical plan dictates that a number of beaches be used, each colored beach may be further divided into beach number one, beach number two, and so forth. When the colored beaches are so divided, the markers are erected in pairs.

HYDROGRAPHIC MARKINGS

8-81. Hydrographic markings have been developed for use near the shore in areas otherwise unsuitable for marking. The shore party commander determines the need for hydrographic markings and installs them. These markings have no relation to Coast Guard aids to navigation. (FM 55-501 describe the navigational aids and the US buoy system.) These are the hydrographic markings for beach operations:

    Rocks, shoals, and submerged obstructions.--

- *Day*--A red and black vertically striped pennant on buoy or stake.
- *Night*--Shielded blue light over red light.

    Boat channel.--

- Right side of channel (from seaward)--
  - *Day*--Red pennant on buoy.
  - *Night*--Shielded red light.
- Left side of channel (from seaward)--

- *Day*--Black pennant on buoy.
- *Night--Shielded white light.*

RANGE MARKERS

8-82. Range markers are two lights or markers located some distance apart and usually visible only from one direction. They are arranged in pairs in line with the center of the channel or the beach. When the operator positions his craft so that the range markers appear one over the other, the craft is on the axis of the channel or on the proper heading to arrive at a designated point on the beach. Characteristics or established ranges are indicated on the hydrographic charts for the particular area.

8-83. When ranges are constructed especially for beach operations, lighter operators get an explanation of their purpose and use in advance. Ranges should be used only after the charts or complete instructions from the water transport unit commander are carefully examined. It is particularly important to determine the distance that a range line can be safely followed. The shore party commander establishes ranges and installs range markers.

COMMUNICATIONS FOR AMPHIBIOUS OPERATIONS

8-84. The physical conditions in amphibious operations require almost complete dependence on radio communication during the initial landings and unloading periods. Because of the large number of radios available in landing force crafts and vehicles and with the combat elements, strict adherence to radio, noise and light discipline is essential. Because of this complexity, land-based communication should be established between shore installations as early as possible. During the initial phases of the operations, the Harbormaster Detachment controls the lighters afloat and the shore party control system controls them ashore. Communication between elements of the water transport units and company headquarters must be planned for and established early in the operation. However, the initial intra-company communications net must be ready to work as soon as the unit control system is established ashore. This net and the control procedures for its use must be provided for during the planning phase.

MAINTENANCE SUPPORT

8-85. During the actual conduct of an amphibious operation, maintenance will be accomplished at the operator/crew (field) level, until additional maintenance capability can be established. Such capability is generally not phased in until the situation ashore is completely established, but will be established as soon as practicable. See the Watercraft Maintenance Chapter for a detailed discussion of Army Watercraft maintenance.

SHORE TO SHORE CROSSING

8-86. Shore-to-shore crossings may use Engineer bridges or modular causeways to transfer personnel and equipment from one shore to another on a river. Army landing craft are used to transfer cargo from one beach terminal to another along the same coastline. Water transport units with small landing craft may be called on to support combat forces conducting shore-to-shore movement or assaults. They may also be requested to ferry cargo across or along rivers and between islands in routine resupply operations. Although shipping is not involved, the operational techniques for water transport units in logistical and tactical shore-to-shore operations are identical to those described in earlier chapters. However, because of the nature of the terrain and the differences in control requirements, some basic planning considerations for shore-to-shore operations and particularly for river crossings are covered in this chapter.

8-87. During tactical shore-to-shore operations, the tactical commander selects the final landing site with the advice of the water transport unit commander. There is normally sufficient time to prepare at the site to ensure mission success. In general, the site selection factors described in Chapter 4 must be considered when evaluating areas for shore-to-shore crossing operations. A factor to consider for river crossing operations in particular, is the location of crossing sites. Crossing sites must be located downstream from bridge sites to reduce the chance of disabled craft and floating debris damaging bridges.

CONTROL POINTS

8-88. Control points normally required for lighterage units in shore-to-shore beach operations are 1) Lighter control center (Harbormaster Detachment), 2) Loading area control point, 3) Near-shore beach control point, 4) Far-shore beach control point, and 5) Discharge control point.

8-89. These points operate in the same manner and fulfill the same functions described in the LOTS chapter. However, the loading area control point replaces the shipboard control point and a beach control point will be added on the far shore. In some cases, it may be expedient to move the lighter control center closer to the waterline and to eliminate the beach control point on the near shore.

ASSEMBLY AREAS

8-90. The commander of the supported unit must consult the commander of the water transport company before designating assembly areas. Desirable characteristics of an assembly area include 1) a Location as near as practicable to the crossing or loading site, 2) Easy entrance from the rear and good exits to the crossing site, 3) Sufficient space to permit dispersion of lighters and provide an adequate loading area, 4) Defiladed so that the enemy cannot observe assembly and maneuver, and 5) Located as near as practicable to a safe harbor or inlet to protect the watercraft in a storm.

RIVERINE OPERATIONS

RIVER CROSSINGS

8-91. Planning for river crossings with bridges or causeways requires careful consideration of the characteristics of the body of water to be crossed. Each bank should have a slope of 40 percent or less. The slope should gradually drop off at the water's edge. Earthmoving equipment may be used to decrease the slope and to level off entrances and exits. Also consider the type and consistency of the soil at the crossing sites; avoid marshy, swampy areas and soils with a clay base. When no hard packed sand entrances and exits are available in the operational area, mobility matting (MoMat), pierced steel planking, brush, and netting may be used to increase traction. Earth-moving equipment may be used to improve the trafficability of the entrance and exit routes at the crossing site. Ideal conditions for a crossing site are a sandy shoreline with a gradual slope; clear, deep water; and a clear river bottom. However, these conditions are not often encountered in the field. Mud is the type of soil usually found in and around rivers.

RIVER CURRENTS

8-92. Operation in rivers with swift currents (more than 2 to 4 knots) requires highly skilled, experienced operators. When exceptionally swift currents are encountered, it may be necessary to rig a cable from one bank to another to assist Engineer craft, Causeway Ferries or Warping Tugs in crossing.

RIVER OBSTACLES

8-93. The most common obstacle on rivers is drifting sandbars. It is unlikely that emplaced obstacles will be encountered in the center of the river, but conventional antitank, antipersonnel, and chemical mines may be laid below the high waterline. Early reconnaissance by the tactical unit should locate mine fields in the area of operations so they can be removed or avoided during crossing. Water transport unit personnel must be trained to look out for mines and to mark and report their location. Use of subsurface obstacle detection technology may also be employed.

8-94. In areas with limited land transportation and abundant water surface, inland waterways provide natural transportation routes. In some developing countries, inland waterways are major arteries for economic circulation. Water routes are strategically and tactically important to an enemy RIVERINE ENVIRONMENT.

8-95. A thorough understanding of riverine environment is needed to plan and conduct riverine operations. In a riverine area, watercraft is the principal means of transport. Civilian waterborne traffic and settlements provide concealment of enemy activity, making control of waterways essential. Water lines of communication (LOC) dominate a riverine environment. Military movements use air and water transportation extensively due to the lack of suitable land transportation networks.

ORGANIZATION AND COMMAND

8-96. Riverine operations can be Joint, e.g., undertaken primarily by Army and Navy forces, or conducted by one Service. Regardless, participating forces must coordinate and integrate efforts to achieve a common objective. Department of Defense (DOD) and Joint Chiefs of Staff (JCS) directives prescribe joint forces command arrangements to ensure coordination and integration. Joint command organizations centrally direct the detailed action of a large number of commands or individuals and common doctrine among the involved forces. Flexibility in the organization ensures control and coordination of these forces in varying operational environments. Considering the total forces available, riverine operations require a balance between types of forces. A special consideration in task organization for riverine operations is the amount of troop lift and fire support available from Navy, Army aviation, and Air Force units. There are several major factors determining maritime support requirements, such as the extent to which navigable waters permit moving maritime support to, within, and around the area of operations, the size of forces to be moved , and the availability of other means of transportation.

SECURITY RESPONSIBILITIES

8-97. The Army and Navy elements assign their appropriate share of forces for local base defense as the base commander directs. The main mission of the Navy force in base defense is to provide gunfire support and protection against any threat from the water. During tactical operations, the Army commander provides, plans, and coordinates security elements (ground or air) along the route of the movement. The Navy element commander tactically controls the movement and maneuver of watercraft under the operational control of the Army commander being supported.

8-98. The Navy commander of the riverine force is responsible for moving Navy ships and watercraft between riverine bases and support facilities outside the riverine area. The Army commander in the riverine area is responsible for the security of movement for ships within the entire operational area.

CONCEPT OF RIVERINE OPERATIONS

8-99. Units conducting riverine operations use water transport extensively to move troops and equipment. Water transport operations normally start from areas where ground forces and watercraft marshal and load and where forces can effect coordination. This may be at a land base next to a navigable waterway, at a Seabase, an afloat base on a navigable waterway, or in an existing area of operations. Once troops or cargo are aboard, the vessels proceed to designated landing areas within an assigned area of operations. Unit plans include control measures, such as phase lines and checkpoints, for the entire operation. The commander controls the unit's movement either from a command and control vessel located within the movement formation, a ground based formation, or from an airborne command post. Maneuver unit commanders, embarked in command and control craft, debark these craft to take charge of their units. The withdrawal of troops from the area of operations is a tactical movement back to the watercraft loading areas. Units are loaded in reverse sequence to that used in the water assault landing. The maneuver unit employing a perimeter security provides the necessary loading area security throughout the withdrawal operation. A tactical water movement back to base areas or to another area of operations is performed after loading.

SUMMARY

8-100. Ability to maneuver combat forces via the maritime domain includes ability to move within and across the littorals into inland waterways. Smaller landing craft can provide this maneuver capability. This was demonstrated by use of Army Landing Craft Mechanized (LCM-8) in the N-hour approach of infantry forces upon the shores of Gamboa, Panama during Operation Just Cause. Movement of combat personnel and supplies is the vital mission provided by the riverine element of Army Watercraft.

Chapter 9

Vessel Convoy Operations

Watercraft units may transport cargo and personnel from shore to shore or sea-base to shore in logistical or tactical support operations. The logistical operation may be conducted to provide facilities or to establish alternate facilities where none previously existed. Tactical support may be conducted to deliver combat ready forces or support forces (air, airborne, or amphibious). It may be under joint or unilateral command. The length of time or the water distance over which landing craft can safely transport troops ashore restricts the range of personnel movements. Under good conditions, a vessel convoy of the current fleet of Army watercraft can travel 80 to 100 miles from sunset to dawn. The JHSV exponentially increases the range and troop carrying capacity of the watercraft fleet by about three times. A designated watercraft unit may be responsible for convoy command and control, navigation and piloting, and defensive measures afloat. Under suitable conditions, various types of small supply vessels or cargo barges and tugboats may also be attached to the watercraft units.

TRACK CHART

9-1.   The vessel unit responsible for the convoy issues a track chart or overlay to each subordinate element. The track chart, prepared from a large-area/small-scale navigation chart, shows the complete route from the assembly area to the objective. Plotting a true course and the distance in nautical miles without deviation shows the route. The route or track is divided into legs at each change of course. Each leg will give true course and nautical miles to the next change of course. At the point of change, a bearing and distance off is shown to some given aid to navigation (either ashore or afloat) for course correction. The using unit makes compass corrections for all courses, using deviation tables for each vessel and the variation shown on the overlay. The unit then determines the speed limit of each vessel within its operating capabilities. The speed to be maintained is computed so that the vessel arrives at the beach objective at a specific time (H-hour or time of arrival). Time of departure is computed by planning backward from the time of arrival and including a small safety factor allowance. The final time determined is the correct time of departure from the assembly area.

NAVIGATIONAL CHART

9-2.   Since navigation is based on the unit track chart, copies of the chart are furnished to the operator of each vessel. Instructions are then available if a vessel becomes separated from its formation. Before the movement begins, navigational instruments must be checked carefully.

9-3.   Preparations include providing COMSEC fills to military communications and navigation devices, Swinging the craft to obtain compass deviations, ensuring that each vessel has a current compass deviation table and that personnel are trained to use the table properly, calibrating signaling equipment, testing and calibrating signaling and listening devices and associated equipment, and checking timepieces, sextants, and all other instruments.

APPROACH CHART

9-4.   When hazardous approaches to a beach present a particularly difficult problem in navigation, an approach chart or overlay is issued to each subordinate vessel element. The chart, prepared on as large a scale as possible, shows:

- Line of departure (for a tactical landing).
- Navigational hazards, including underwater obstacles.

- Courses to avoid. Vessels may have to land in small groups or singularly. The approach may require changing course with several shifts in direction between the far shore assembly area and the beach.

- Formations required.

- Hydrographic obstructions, narrow channels, wharfs, and the speed and direction of unusual currents.

- Panoramic sketches or oblique aerial photographs of the beach seen from seaward supplement the approach chart. Identifying points are marked on the photographs.

NAVIGATIONAL METHODS

9-5.   The navigational methods used to guide a convoy vary with the availability of navigational aids and charts, ocean currents, visibility, and the configuration of the ocean bottom. In a tactical operation, the position of the leading command and navigation vessel must be known accurately to within 100 to 200 yards when within 1 to 3 miles of the enemy shore. This degree of accuracy is difficult to obtain, especially if the movement is at night.

9-6.   Electronic signal devices secretly planted on or near the enemy shore by other agencies or units are often used to guide the lead vessel, which picks up the signals with its receiving equipment. Another method is to place personnel ashore by rubber boat or parachute to show, at a specified time, a shielded light. A beam radio or invisible-light transmitter may be set up to guide the navigational vessel. However, radio silence is jeopardized when wireless transmitting devices are used.

9-7.   Regardless of the far-shore aids that may be installed, the navigator still must depend largely on conventional methods of navigation. Electronic Chart Display Information System (ECDIS) has Global Positioning System (GPS) input and can provide very accurate navigation information. However, reliance upon a single system is imprudent. Proper allowance for currents must be made; depth-finder soundings must be plotted on charts. The effective range of radar equipment in the convoy depends on the type of radar set used and the height of the antenna above the surface of the water. A constant radar plot is maintained both to check the accuracy of electronic navigational equipment and to keep a check on the convoy formation.

9-8.   Two vessels may work together to establish a route into an otherwise unmarked area. One vessel, far enough ahead to reconnoiter by depth finder, sonar, hand-lead line or other means, establishes a buoy to mark a designated location. The second vessel guiding the formation homes in on the buoy. To use this method requires good charts. If visibility is sufficient, the navigator can take bearings on various land features as the far shore is approached, or radar ranges, if so equipped. These objectives must be known in relation to the landing area. This may involve running parallel to the beach until a sufficient number of points are recognized to establish a position and to set a course for the beach.

VESSEL CONTROL

9-9.   While the operation is being planned, the vessel's navigation officer and a representative of the terminal headquarters (or other unit responsible for far-shore operations) thoroughly study landing conditions. The Terminal headquarters coordinator for vessel operations is the Harbormaster Detachment. Tentative plans for vessel and beach control are agreed on, including the location of landing points for craft. In a shore-to-shore operation, the vessel control officer:

- Controls the movement of all craft between the near and far shore.

- Marks control points to regulate vessel movements and other points designated by the higher headquarters.

- Informs the commander of the vessel unit of the movement's progress.

EMBARKATION

9-10. The Harbormaster operations cell of the battalion, along with the headquarters of the units being transported, prepares an assembly chart or an overlay on a small-scale navigation chart. The chart shows true courses and distances in nautical miles from the dispersal areas to the rendezvous areas, from the rendezvous areas to the embarkation points, from the embarkation points to the regulating point, and from the regulating point to a final convoy formation in the assembly area. The assembly chart is prepared similarly to the track chart. An assembly table may accompany the assembly chart. The table prescribes times of departure from the embarkation points and the regulating point. It also gives the specific times of arrival for vessel units or landing teams in the assembly areas. Vessels are queued on the near shore until they are required to form for embarkation/loading. If possible, the arrival of each craft at the shore is synchronized with the arrival of the troops and supplies. (The time required to load troops and supplies must be considered by the unit being transported and the vessel unit assigned to the movement.) To avoid undue fatigue, troops are loaded at the latest possible hour that permits the convoy to depart at the designated time. Troop movement should be aboard vessels designed to carry passengers, such as JHSV or LCM-8, Mod 2. After loading, they proceed to designated rendezvous areas offshore. Rendezvous areas are assigned for vessels assigned to the convoy. Vessels are directed to the assembly area location that they will occupy in the convoy. Using the track chart, they then proceed in prescribed formation to the far shore.

CONVOY ORGANIZATION

9-11. The convoy is formed in waves or elements of six to eight vessels, depending on the landing plan. The convoy commander is normally the senior vessel master in the convoy. The convoy commander's vessel heads the formation and controls the vessel formation and route. The commander of embarked troops travels in the same vessel as the convoy commander. Control vessels are stationed on the flanks. A salvage vessel follows in the rear.

CONVOY FORMATION

9-12. The formations used within a convoy vary according to the situation. They depend on such factors as the tactical plan (for a tactical landing), weather, time of day, sea conditions, phase of the operation (whether the convoy is en route to the far shore or approaching the beach for the landing), and Enemy situation and capabilities (including nuclear).

9-13. Generally, a convoy moves in a column formation upon arrival in the landing area. The distance between vessels, stern to bow, should be no less than 0.5 nm apart, depending on visibility. In poor weather, craft must travel further apart and closely monitor craft in close proximity. To avoid collisions, they should not move closer than one vessel length apart when operating in close quarters.

9-14. The closed-V formation provides excellent control. It permits rapid deployment into an open-V formation in case of air attack. The open-V and line-abreast formations are used to approach the beach before landing. However, they are difficult to control. Normally, they are used only for short distances. The line-abreast formation is normally used only in a landing (usually tactical) where all vessels must beach at the same time. When radio silence must be observed, code flag signals or flashing light using Morse code may be used to pass maneuvering signals between vessels. Vessel master are trained in use of flashing light with Morse code.

COMMAND AND CONTROL

9-15. The convoy commander is responsible for the control of craft, navigation, mitigation of risk, and coordination of local defensive measures. He or she must:

- Ensure that all landing craft arrive and depart from the embarkation points on time.

- Ensure that craft are in the prescribed formations and depart from assembly areas on time with minimal confusion and delay.

- Provide accurate navigation from the near shore to the landing area so that craft arrive on time and in prescribed formations.

- Patrol the convoy to maintain formation and help craft having difficulties.

- Establish control vessels ahead of the formation to direct the landing.

- Control the movement to the beach and the landing of craft.

- Conduct a comprehensive risk assessment of convoy operations.

To assist the convoy in conducting operations, one higher headquarters liaison officer should be designated to coordinate vessel activities to support combatant commander maneuver requirements.

CONVOY CONTROL

9-16. The distance between craft and poor visibility may complicate the control of vessel units in convoy. Visual communication must be highly efficient since radios must be kept free for traffic other than control messages. Voice-amplifying equipment is desirable for all control and salvage vessels. Leaders of small vessel units must ensure that coxswains maintain their positions in the prescribed formation and follow specified speeds. Night operations are particularly difficult and physically and mentally strain personnel. Strict compliance with regulations concerning authorized lights is essential. A single unauthorized light may cause general confusion in the convoy movement. Bow lights on top of the LCM ramp are turned off because they tend to blind the coxswain. A lookout is posted in the bow to watch for hazards, and night-vision devices or forward-looking sonar may be employed. Control vessels are used to prevent straggling, assist vessels in trouble, and aid in navigational control. They patrol the flanks and rear of the formation and communicate with the navigator. Control vessels (picket boats) may also serve as messenger boats. If possible, the formation should proceed to a safe haven before the onset of bad weather. If the control officer believes that further movement would be hazardous, he may order the convoy to move into a predetermined closed formation with the control vessel in the center. The craft maintain enough way to keep their positions.

APPROACH TO LANDING AREA

9-17. Command and navigation vessels and picket boats make up navigational control points and hazards. In a tactical operation, they also mark the rendezvous area and the line of departure. Picket boats may precede the convoy, establishing submerged or floating buoys, invisible-light transmitters, and other devices to mark control points, obstructions, and channels. Aircraft and submarines may also be used for this purpose. An initial point may be designated about 10 miles offshore to guide the vessel formations to the rendezvous area for tactical landings. The position of the initial point depends on the distance between the near and far shores. It should be far enough from the landing area to allow the entire convoy to rearrange time schedules if necessary. The convoy may be delayed at the initial point if it is ahead of schedule or if any rearrangements are needed in the existing formation. In a tactical landing, when the convoy enters the rendezvous area, the designated control vessels move out to their stations and mark the line of departure. The waves assemble and are ordered to the line of departure according to an approach schedule.

CONVOY SECURITY

9-18. Fighter aircraft, Army aircraft, Navy vessels, or armed landing craft may protect the convoy. Vessels in the convoy should be equipped with weapons suitable for antiaircraft and anti-vessel defense. Army watercraft may be modified locally according to the requirements of the situation and the armament available. Landing craft may also transport tanks; landing vehicles, tracked, armored; or self-propelled guns to provide defensive firepower in support of an assault landing. Weapons and ammunition in a craft are kept available at all times, and sentinels are always on duty. In the first hours of the voyage, alert warning systems are tested and rehearsed.

9-19. Each vessel is assigned a sector for observation and defense. In case of attack, vessels deploy into prearranged open formations. They must avoid becoming so scattered that communication and control are lost. All available weapons are fired against attacking airplanes or vessels.

9-20. Each control vessel section closely inspects the appropriate beach area immediately after landing. Section members determine the type of bottom; the depth of water; the location of rocks, boulders, shoals, bars, sunken wrecks, and other obstacles; the nature of any crosscurrents; and other pertinent information. After the salvage vessel arrives, it helps to reconnoiter the water approaches and to determine the depth of water offshore. The control vessel section or personnel of the shore party (if the landing is tactical) mark and remove all hazards to navigation. Pennants placed on buoys or stakes mark hazards that cannot be removed. The control vessel sections of the appropriate shore party unit must keep the beach clear. Stranded vessels, vehicles, supplies, and debris must not be allowed to block landing points. To control vessel traffic, members of the control vessel section signal landing craft to the proper landing place. Coxswains get directions concerning proper angle of approach, speed, beaching lowering of ramp, unloading, and retraction. Since it is often difficult for a coxswain to determine the exact location of a beach landing site, a flagman stands in the center of the site and guides the beaching craft. Guidance is particularly necessary for craft that are transporting vehicles. Range markers help the coxswain approach the beaching site.

EMERGENCY MAINTENANCE & SALVAGE

9-21. Maintenance personnel, equipment, and repair parts are distributed throughout the convoy. In addition, each company salvage boat is stationed at the rear of its company formation. This position enables observation of any crafts that may need help. The salvage boat also acts as a rescue boat. As the convoy leaves the near shore, the salvage boat assists where needed and does not depart until the last craft is under way. Each salvage boat carries a specially trained crew. A prearranged signal indicates when a landing craft needs assistance. The salvage boat assists vessels in distress as much as possible. However, under no circumstances does it lose contact with the formation. Salvage boat mechanics make minor engine repairs, supply replacement parts, or give the engineman instructions so he can correct the malfunction and get under way. However, repairs requiring considerable time are refused. The salvage boat serves the entire formation. It cannot leave the formation to service individual vessels. The salvage boat may tow the disabled craft until repairs are made, or a mechanic may be left to make repairs. A control vessel may tow the craft or may transfer troops from the disabled craft to another landing craft. If available, empty LCMs are included in the convoy for use in emergencies.

9-22. The salvage boat and at least one landing craft in each wave usually carry towlines. The lines should be of appropriate breaking strength for towing, at least 200 feet long and equipped with bridles and adequate chafing gear. The bridles should be designed so that they maybe secured to the mooring bitts of the towed and towing craft. At the landing area, salvage boats may cruise around the area, alert to assist where needed, or they may anchor at a location to observe all craft.

This page intentionally left blank.

Chapter 10

Watercraft Maintenance

Maintenance tasks include any action that sustains material in an operational condition, restores it to a fully mission-capable (FMC) condition, or upgrades it through modification or product improvement. Tasks range from simple Preventive Maintenance Checks and Services (PMCS) of equipment to complex depot operations performed in fixed shop facilities.

The Army Maintenance System consists of two categories or levels, Field and Sustainment. FM 4-30.3 specifically outlines how these levels are implemented at the operational and tactical level. Refer to FM 4-30.3 for doctrinal guidance for conducting Army watercraft maintenance. More detail can be found in this chapter, training circulars and vessel technical manuals. Basic tenets of two-level maintenance are these: field maintenance is primarily characterized by "on-system" maintenance that repairs and returns equipment to the operator or the user. Sustainment maintenance is characterized by "off-system" maintenance that primarily repairs and returns equipment and components to the supply system. For vessels, the field maintenance can be described as on-craft maintenance and repair and return of subcomponents. Sustainment maintenance will be a combination of on and off-craft maintenance for items and the majority of those tasks previously designated as Depot level. The Two-Level system replaces the old Four-level system, resulting in a reduction of resources requirements by eliminating duplication at each echelon.

ARMY WATERCRAFT MAINTENANCE

10-1. The objective of Army watercraft maintenance is to ensure safe, seaworthy, reliable watercraft. The major functional responsibilities of the Army watercraft maintenance activities are:

- Sustaining the vessels in an operational status.

- Restoring them to a serviceable condition.

- Updating or upgrading its functional usefulness through Modification Work Orders (MWO), materiel change, and product improvement.

- Maintaining equipment to Technical Manual (TM) –10 and –20 series standards.

10-2. Field maintenance actions are typically defined as on system maintenance and involve replacement of Class IX components, on-system adjustments, supporting repair and return to the user and is performed at all echelons. Inspections at the crew and unit level are the first step in determining required maintenance issues and repairs. The crew then works on reducing and eliminating discrepancies and identifies field-level repair actions requiring additional parts, tools and manpower that may be provided by the Watercraft Field Maintenance Company (WFMC). Arrangements are made with the designated support element at the Watercraft Inspection Branch (WIB) for sustainment maintenance support.

10-3. Sustainment work order requests will be processed through the field maintenance companies or respective AMSA shops until future reorganization of the WFMCs is complete and Standard Army Management Information System (STAMIS) system software upgrades have been implemented. Field level maintenance tasks will be accomplished at the lowest level possible and proper man hour/parts accounting captured in SAMS-1E by MSTs and or company maintenance personnel. Field level maintenance repairs will not be accomplished at sustainment maintenance facilities during OCCM unless prior coordination and approval have been given by the Chief of Watercraft Inspection Branch (CWIB). All approved field level repairs will be entirely funded by the requesting command.

10-4. The procedures for requesting sustainment level maintenance of all Army watercraft through the watercraft national maintenance point (WNMP) are as follows: All requests for sustainment maintenance are accomplished through the SAMS-1E automated process using DA 5990-E work request form. Manual forms may only be used when the automated system is not available or in emergency situations; however, when manual forms are used the work order will be entered into SAMS-1E at the earliest opportunity for maintenance tracking. Commanders ensure all maintenance activities adhere to guidelines set forth by TACOM through the WIB in their current external SOP. This includes all pre-on condition cyclic maintenance (OCCM) surveys, OCCM, warranty claims, interim OCCM surveys, un-programmed repairs, and emergency maintenance requests. Emergency repairs will not be delayed for work order submission but will be required no later than completion of emergency repairs. Procedures for submission of sustainment level work orders will be dictated by TACOM through the WIB external SOP and AR 750-1.

10-5. Maintenance that requires extensive resources such as special equipment, machinery or dry-dock facilities characterizes watercraft Sustainment Maintenance. Under certain conditions, such as when a short-notice mission occurs and the vessel is in a non-operational status, the vessel's Chief Engineer is authorized to direct the crew to affect a sustainment level repair. In order to do so, several conditions must exist - the field-level operators or maintainers must have the training to conduct the repair, the parts must be on hand, and the tools must be available, and TACOM must approve the repair.

10-6. Sustainment Maintenance of watercraft is a Title 46 of the U.S. Code responsibility and is defined as a "depot level service" involving a series of inspections, certifications and condition based maintenance actions that are designed to ensure that a watercraft's structure, machinery, and other equipment are maintained in an operational, seaworthy and safe condition. The major components of watercraft sustainment maintenance are the actions and functions grouped under the term On Condition Cyclic Maintenance (OCCM). The primary focus of OCCM includes dry-docking, bottom cleaning, underwater painting, overhauls, replacement of major components, application of major Modification Work Orders (MWOs), emergency repairs, load line, and quadrennial certifications, and all those actions formerly known as "interval depot maintenance."

10-7. WIB provides an annual schedule for all watercraft due OCCM to commands with watercraft assets. Units with watercraft due OCCM during the upcoming year generate a pre-OCCM work order requesting OCCM survey inspection no later than 180 days of the shipyard due date or 18 months after the vessel's last refloat for interim OCCM surveys. It is the responsibility of the unit to submit a sustainment level work request to initiate action from WIB for this survey. WIB will host a pre-OCCM round table meeting to discuss results of the pre-OCCM survey and a follow on round table at a location and method of their choice to ensure completion of all field maintenance prior to start of OCCM.

10-8. The maintenance strategy is defined by a combination of on-station and shipyard maintenance that is defined by three distinct, but integrated functions within a vessel's operational cycle: phased maintenance, annual maintenance and inspections & certifications. These phases are described in detail in FM 4-30.3.

10-9. Before a vessel is accepted into sustainment maintenance, units/crews are required to complete all field level maintenance tasks identified during the pre-shipyard Technical Inspection (TI). The watercraft field maintenance unit helps bridge manning shortfalls to achieve this. Units are responsible for funding all field level maintenance not associated with a sustainment level task. It is not cost effective to leave tasks undone during a sustainment maintenance period. Vessel Masters, Chief Engineers and appropriate members of the crew as determined by the chain of command, in accordance with AR 56-9, will accompany their vessels to the shipyard during sustainment maintenance periods. As a minimum, Vessel Masters and Chief Engineers will accompany vessels to the shipyard. This becomes the identified crew members' places of duty. Their responsibility during this period is to assist the WIB Marine Surveyor with vessel-related matters, capture and record demand data related to maintenance man-hour information for field level maintenance performed and repair parts installed during the maintenance period.

10-10. Watercraft safety equipment, including firefighting, dewatering, and lifesaving equipment, is maintained by the crew in accordance with FM 4-01.502, Army Watercraft Safety. Hard-mounted, wired systems that are an inherent part of the vessel are maintained by a combination of operator/crew for field-level and TACOM

WIB for sustainment level. For example, the general alarm system may be tested by the crew, but the wiring of the system may require sustainment level repair.

10-11. Army watercraft are sustained, restored, updated or upgraded, and maintained through (PMCS) and (Phase Maintenance). Phase maintenance is the sustainment level (depot) maintenance that ensures compliance with international and national maritime regulatory guidance for minimum safety standards at sea.

Note: Vessels in storage are stored in accordance with TB 740-97-4 (Preservation, Storage & Depreservation of Watercraft) at 10/20 standards IAW AR 750-1 and FM 3-35.1 but will require activation. Pre-positioned and LBE vessels require periodic maintenance and operation of critical systems and subsystems, annual technical inspections and certifications. Under the maintenance statuses outlined in FM 4-30.3, they are reported as fully mission capable (FMC).

10-12. Maintenance and operations are inextricably linked. The maintenance status of a vessel or vessels impacts and drives a unit's ability to perform its mission. Operations and maintenance must be linked throughout organizational constructs. Operations personnel must continually communicate with maintenance personnel to manage and influence maintenance operations, and subsequently the operational posture of the organization. This information must flow smoothly between each level of responsibility. Operations and maintenance information originates with the individual vessels.

10-13. Vessel crews manage their operational and maintenance status and provide this information to the units' Vessel Support Office (VSO) on a daily basis. The VSO consolidates the information, provides assistance and resources within its ability and provides the status to the Harbormaster Operations Detachment (HMOD). The HMOD was designed and intended to provide a battalion, Transportation Terminal or higher command, with the ability and expertise to monitor both the operations and maintenance status of Army watercraft. The HMOD coordinates and monitors maintenance information with the VSOs and the supporting field maintenance organizations and provides this status to the battalion operations staff who then forwards the information to the Sustainment Brigade's Transportation Theater Opening Element (TTOE). The TTOE contains the Sustainment Brigades terminal operations and watercraft operations expertise.

Table 10-1. Maintenance Intervals

	Vessel	Inspections & Certifications	Run Ups, Trials & Annual Maintenance	Phased Maintenance
AC & RC	All Vessels Except BCs & BDs	Annual	Annual (Maint only)	Every 3 Years
	BD	Annual	Annual (Maint only)	Every 4 Years
	BC	Annual	Annual	Every 5 Years
APS	BD 115T	Weekly, Monthly, Annual	Monthly & Annual	Every 4 Years
	Wet Stored - LCU & LT	Weekly, Monthly, Annual	Quarterly & Annual	Every 5 Years
	Dry Stored - BG, LCM, ST, MWT & SLWT	Weekly, Monthly, Annual	Quarterly, Semi-Annual & Annual	Every 6 Years

10-14. Phase maintenance begins with a Materiel Condition Survey (MCS) performed 180 days prior to the scheduled phase maintenance cycle. This survey provides the basis for written specifications by which Phase Maintenance is accomplished. This is a dockside inspection utilizing the services of qualified divers when possible to ascertain the condition of the watercraft's hull and appendages below the deep load waterline. A second MCS is performed at the time of dry-docking to identify additional repair/maintenance requirements not observable at the time of the 180–day inspection. These inspections are performed at the direction of the TACOM WIB with assistance from the American Bureau of Shipping (ABS) as required by law. Maintenance intervals for all vessels are shown in Table 10-1.

STORED VESSEL MAINTENANCE

10-15. A stored vessel is a pre-positioned vessel or operational vessel placed in extended command-designated administrative storage. Vessels in storage are stored at 10/20 standards IAW AR 750-1 but will require activation. Pre-positioned and LBE vessels require periodic (weekly, monthly, semi-annual) maintenance to critical systems and sub-systems, annual technical inspections and re-certifications.

EXERCISING VESSELS

10-16. Vessels are "exercised" to maintain and verify readiness. Exercise is defined as a minimum of eight (8) continuous hours with all vessel systems and subsystems operating as if underway. Complete all annual certifications and recertification required to maintain regulatory compliance. Exercise of Barge Derrick (BD) requires recertification of quadrennial permit, exercise of all hoists through 100% range of motion, with a minimum 25% working load.

10-17. Prior to exercising a vessel: MWOs are completed and Hull husbandry is conducted.

10-18. The scope of work accomplished during Phase Maintenance varies, depending upon watercraft condition, resource limitations, class of vessel, and other factors. As a minimum, the following maintenance and repair actions are accomplished during Phase Maintenance:

- Bottom cleaning and painting up to the deep-load waterline per TB 43–0144.

- All repairs below the deep-load waterline as identified during dry-dock inspection/underwater hull survey.

- Overhaul/replacement/renewal of all major components identified for overhaul at the depot level as determined through diagnostic testing, hours of operation, and inspection of internal components.

10-19. All other maintenance and/or repairs identified by the marine/ship surveyor required to affect a permanent change in the watercraft's condition, to ensure capability of operating in an unrestricted manner for the purposes intended, capability of being maintained and operated per all applicable regulations, rules, laws, and policies, sustainability of the inherent reliability and maintainability designed and manufactured into the equipment between repair cycles, and sustainability of acceptable rates of watercraft readiness between phase maintenance cycles.

10-20. All minimum maritime safety inspections, tests and drills required by Army Watercraft are listed in AR 56-9, including those required by regulatory documents of ABS; 46 CFR 41–69; and International Convention for Safety of Life at Sea, 1974 (SOLAS) to maintain the load-line documentation in a current status.

COSIS (CARE OF SUPPLIES IN STORAGE) MAINTENANCE

10-21. COSIS maintenance encompasses all aspects of field level maintenance and initiation of all sustainment maintenance actions. Every effort shall be made to incorporate MWOs, Maintenance Advisory Messages (MAM), and Safety of Use Messages (SOUM) during exercise periods.

INSPECTIONS AND CERTIFICATIONS

10-22. Unit commanders/maintenance managers are responsible for initiating all required tests, inspections, and certifications and will correct deficiencies that may prevent certification. Annual inspections may be conducted during phase or condition based maintenance, when determined by TACOM to be more advantageous to the Army.

10-23. TACOM Watercraft Inspection Branch (WIB) will monitor and report compliance with test, inspection and certification requirements. Inspections and certifications include but are not limited to:

- Annual fixed firefighting systems.

- Annual load test of all lifting devices.

- Annual revalidation of quadrennial inspections.

- Annual load line inspection.

- Life rafts.

- Hydrostatic releases.

- Self Contained Breathing Apparatus (SCBA).

- Compressed Air pressure vessels.

- Boilers.

- Confined Space Entry equipment.

- TMDE.

- Radio Stations.

- Annual DOD Information Assurance Certification and Accreditation Process (DIACAP).

WARRANTY CLAIMS

10-24. Owning units will be given a memorandum and supporting documents identifying the warranty beginning and end dates. The warranty shall identify any specific items with a warranty deviating from the standard 90-day warranty period. Watercraft warranty claims will be processed through the nearest TACOM WIB field support offices.

10-25. Warranties for Army Watercraft shall start at government acceptance in accordance with AR 700-139, Army Warranty Programs. Components acquired in performance of field or sustainment operations or MWOs shall have warranties IAW with AR 700-139.

WATERCRAFT MAINTENANCE ORGANIZATIONS

10-26. The watercraft field maintenance company consists of modular maintenance teams capable of deploying worldwide in support of deployed watercraft with a modified modular tool set stocked with watercraft-specific parts and special tools. For maximum effectiveness, the watercraft maintenance unit is assigned to brigade or higher as part of a theater opening/port opening package.

10-27. Army Watercraft field maintenance organizations and procedures consist of:

- Onboard vessel equipment and crew capable of performing maintenance and repairs while underway.

- A modular maintenance surge team located within the same theater of operations, ashore or at a sea-base capable of performing maintenance tasks not able to be performed underway or that requires additional personnel, fault correction, condition-based repair, or replacement.

10-28. The Watercraft Field Maintenance Company (WFMC) is trained and equipped to provide field level maintenance to all Army watercraft. Funding is provided by the supporting command (i.e., FORSCOM). Unit personnel formed into field maintenance platoons that are divided into squad sized Maintenance Support Teams (MSTs). These MSTs can and will deploy aboard Army vessels to provide additional man-hours for field level preventative and unscheduled maintenance. They will also perform sustainment level maintenance tasks when authorized.

10-29. Sustainment level tasks are normally the responsibility of TACOM. However, this responsibility will fall to the vessel Chief Engineer when craft are individually deployed, and the higher HQ's Marine Maintenance Officer (MMO) when the WFMC is deployed. The MSTs deploy with an expeditionary shelter (providing in-transit billeting and administrative space when required) and a mobile contact vehicle for mobility. Once on station, the expeditionary shelters may be consolidated ashore to provide the MST office and billet space. When required, the WFMC will deploy the Headquarters maintenance operations section and maintenance support teams together via air, sea or a combination of deployment methods. The WFMC HQ will deploy with expeditionary shelters providing work and storage space ashore and power generation capability, as METT-TC requires.

10-30. Command & Control relationships will vary and develop as METT-TC dictates. When the WFMC is deployed en masse, the MSTs will be under the command and control of the unit HQ's. When the company HQ is not deployed and multiple maintenance support teams are onboard vessels operational or tactical control may transfer to a (HMOD) as mission dictates. When deployed independently aboard a vessel an MST receives its direction from the Vessel Master/Chief Engineer. The team may also be under tactical or operational control of a watercraft unit or detachment when the watercraft unit/detachment is deployed in total and an MST is deployed individually.

10-31. TACOM is responsible for ensuring adequate support worldwide for the accomplishment of sustainment maintenance and support during unforecasted system failures that are beyond the capability of the crew. Coordination for sustainment level maintenance support is accomplished through one of several means. The WFMC coordinates directly with the TACOM Watercraft Inspection Branch (WIB) when the entire company is deployed, much like the home station process. Alternatively, when several MSTs are deployed without the company HQ's the HMOD can request support via the TACOM WIB representative or reach back capability. When vessels are deployed independently the vessel's Chief Engineer can coordinate directly for TACOM support.

10-32. The conduit for watercraft units to access sustainment maintenance capabilities is the TACOM (WIB). The WIB functions as the technical advisor and Contracting Officer's Representative (COR) during sustainment maintenance. It does not, in and of itself, have the physical capability to perform sustainment maintenance actions. Watercraft units access these capabilities through the normal SAMS-E work order process. The WIB is responsible for arranging and managing OCCM or Sustainment maintenance for all vessels. They can, under certain conditions, provide support to complete field level maintenance.

WATERCRAFT MAINTENANCE MANAGEMENT AND REPORTING

10-33. Vessels not already equipped, that will be operating independently or in a task force, will request a SAM **Maintenance Management**. STAMIS will continue to support Army watercraft maintenance, but with an enhanced level of support. All Class A vessels; Joint High Speed Vessels (JHSV), Logistics Support Vessels (LSV), Landing Craft Utility 2000 class (LCU-2000), and Large Tugs will be provided with an on-board Standard Army Maintenance System – Enhanced (SAMS-E) computer. This system will be used both while operating from home port and while deployed. The difference will be to whom they provide their data. Operating from home port, the supply request data will be transmitted to the supporting SSA for management and accountability, who will in turn process the requisition. While deployed, the vessel will transmit the data directly to the source of supply for shipment. Military Sources of Supply (SOS), local vendors, and private companies are researched by the crew or other maintenance activity for geographic location of potential suppliers of critical systems in the deployment area of operations and enroute. Requisitions will be shipped directly to the vessel's deployed location or to the next port of call. The shore based unit provides the derivative UIC and Routing Identifier Code (RIC) for underway Class A vessels and will provide oversight and management of those requisitions via ILAP except for JHAV and LSV which are detachments and do not require derivative UICs.. The vessels will manage their own supply assets while underway. Class B vessels; Landing Craft Mechanized, (LCM), Small Tugs (ST), Barge Derrick Cranes (BD), and Modular Causeway Systems (MCS) will remain dependent upon their organizational maintenance and supply assets for support. These vessels are harbor craft and do not have the capability to support stand alone systems; nor do they have the communications systems needed to operate remotely. However, they will use the SAMS-E "Logbook" or similar feature to record and submit their maintenance and supply data electronically. Figure 10-1 illustrates the flow of SAMS-E information and functions.

10-34. Vessels not already equipped, that will be operating independently or in a task force, will request a SAMS-1E computer through its chain of command to the Army G-4 to provide it or the watercraft task force remote maintenance management and supply support while deployed.

10-35. Readiness reporting is completed from the platform crew through Life Cycle Management Command (LCMC) levels via a combined system of manual and automated methods IAW DA Pam 750-8, The Army Maintenance Management System (TAMMS) Users Manual.

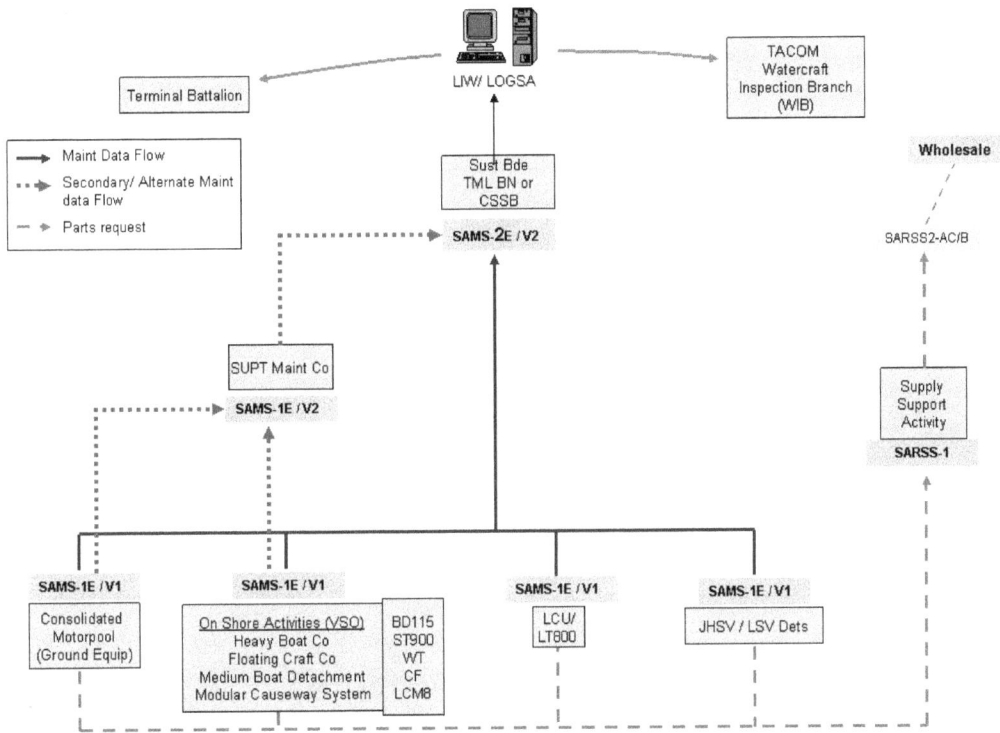

FIGURE 10-1. Readiness Reporting

FUTURE/TRANSITIONAL MAINTENANCE

10-36. New system requirements must be standard throughout the fleet, implemented on new builds, and retrofitted to current systems to maintain DOD interoperability, supportability, and readiness. One of these systems is Condition Based Maintenance (CBM).

10-37. The use of CBM is a transformational change in the scheduling, performance, management and, more importantly, the impact of maintenance on readiness and combat power. The transition to CBM for designated equipment will affect Army watercraft through its fundamental reliance on enabling technologies.

10-38. The intent of CBM is to reduce maintenance down time and increase operational readiness by repairing or replacing system components based on the actual condition of the component as opposed to other maintenance concepts, such as scheduled or time-phased maintenance procedures. CBM will eliminate as many scheduled maintenance actions as can be done without compromising safety. This allows maintenance resources to be focused on readiness tasks and is in step with the concept of a reduced support footprint.

10-39. For Army Watercraft, CBM will replace DS/GS level contracted maintenance for in-port, pier side maintenance on an as-needed basis, but no less than annually.

10-40. Although being established as a standard for maintenance in the Army, it is envisioned that only selected items of Army equipment (approved under an Army decision process) will be converted to the full CBM model, complete with complex sensor suites and real time data transmission to information and command and control systems. Attaining full operational capability for Army CBM will take a number of years.

Chapter 11

Watercraft Accident Reporting and Investigation

Reporting and investigating watercraft accidents in a complete and timely manner is extremely important. This chapter gives guidance to leadership on when to investigate watercraft accidents and to write accident reports involving Army watercraft. Detailed instructions information may be found in FM 4-01.502 *Watercraft Safety*, AR 385-10, AR 56-9, and DA Pamphlet 385-40.

This manual covers watercraft under DA jurisdiction that are:

- Operated, controlled or directed by the Army. This includes watercraft furnished by a contractor or another government agency when operated by Army watercraft personnel.

- Loaned or leased to non-Army organizations for modification, maintenance, repair, test, or for contractor research or development projects for the Army.

- Under test by Army agencies responsible for research, development, and testing of equipment.

- Under operational control of a contractor for the Army.

WATERCRAFT ACCIDENT

11-1. A watercraft accident is an unplanned event or series of events, involving watercraft under DA jurisdiction that results in one or more of the following:

- Accidents occurring while loading, off-loading, or receiving services at dockside.

- Damage to Army property (including government-furnished material, government property, or government-furnished equipment provided to a contractor).

- Accidents occurring during amphibious or on-shore warfare training.

- Fatal or nonfatal injury to military personnel on or off duty.

- Fatal or nonfatal injury to on-duty Army civilian personnel, including non-appropriated fund employees and foreign nationals employed by the Army, incurred during performance of duties while in a work compensable status.

- Fatal or nonfatal occupational injury or illness to Army military personnel, Army civilian employees, non-appropriated fund employees, or foreign nationals employed by the Army.

- Fatal or nonfatal injury or illness to non-Army personnel or damage to non-Army property.

11-2. Watercraft accidents do not include accidents that are reportable as aviation (Class E or F) accidents or incidents. When two or more type vehicles are involved (i.e. An LCM and a Stryker), the type of equipment operated by the individual deemed the most responsible will determine the accident type.

REASONS TO INVESTIGATE AND REPORT ACCIDENTS

11-3. Watercraft accidents are reported and investigated to identify problem areas (deficiencies) as early as possible in order to prevent further damage to equipment or loss/injury of personnel. Changes, corrections, and countermeasures can be developed and implemented. If an accident is never reported, the local command and required DA agencies will not know there is a problem. Unreported accidents lead to repeat occurrences.

WHAT TO REPORT AND INVESTIGATE

11-4. All watercraft accidents must be reported by the master/operator, regardless of class, to the local command, commands of concern, and Transportation Branch Marine Safety Office at marinesafety@conus.army.mil within 24 hours of occurrence via any electronic means available. This may also be done telephonically. The local command must insure the Transportation Branch Marine Safety Office and Commander, USACRC are notified if not previously reported by the master/operator. Commander USACRC may be notified through the Web-based initial notification (IN) tool on the USACRC website at https://crc.army.mil/home.

11-5. Only certain accidents require completion and submission of DA Form 285 (US Army Accident Report) by the Investigating Officer. These recordable accidents include Classes A, B, C, and D accidents (see AR 385-10 for details).

11-6. The Army classifies accidents by severity of injury and property damage. These classes (A through D) are used to determine the appropriate investigative and reporting procedures.

11-7. Class A accident has a total cost of reportable damage of $1,000,000 or more; destroys an Army aircraft, watercraft, missile, or spacecraft; or has an occupational illness that results in a fatality or permanent total disability.

11-8. Class B accident has a total cost of reportable property damage of $200,000 or more, but less than $1,000,000; an injury and/or occupational illness that results in permanent partial disability, or three (3) or more people hospitalized as inpatients.

11-9. Class C accident has a total cost of property damage of $20,000 or more, but less than $200,000; a nonfatal injury that causes one (1) or more days away from work or training beyond the day or shift on which it occurred; or a disability at any time (lost time case).

11-10. Class D accident has a cost of property damage of $2,000 or more, but less than $20,000; or a nonfatal injury or illness resulting in restricted work, transfer to another job, medical treatment greater than first aid, needle stick injuries and cuts from sharps that are contaminated with another person's blood or other potentially infectious material, medical removal under medical surveillance requirements of an OSHA standard, occupational hearing loss, or a work-related tuberculosis case.

NOTE: Property damage is defined as the cost to repair or replace. Property damage costs are separated from personnel injury/illness costs for classifying A through C accidents.

RESPONSIBILITIES

11-11. **Vessel Master/Operator:** Record details, and report the accident as soon as possible in as outlined in FM 4-01.502 Watercraft Safety.

11-12. **Local chain of command:** Ensures all required notifications are made.

11-13. Commander with general court martial jurisdiction (OR unit responsible for operation, personnel or materiel involved in the accident): For accidents requiring a DA Form 285, appoints an investigating officer.

11-14. Investigating Officer:

- Preserves evidence and conducts the investigation IAW DA Pam 385-40.
- Fills out the detailed DA Form 285 report.

- Forwards DA Form 285 through the installation safety office to the Army Safety Center for recording in the Army Safety Management Information System (ASMIS) within 30 days of the accident.

- (When applicable) Sends Army Reserve reports to Army Reserve Safety Directorate at: Commander, USARC, ATTN: ARRC-SA, 1401 Deshler St SW, Fort McPherson, GA 30330.

ADDITIONAL REPORT REQUIREMENTS FOR GROUNDED VESSELS

11-15. In addition to the DA Form 285 report, watercraft accidents invoking grounding that creates a hazard to navigation or watercraft safety or any occurrence that affects the watercraft's seaworthiness or fitness for service (including, but not limited to fire, flooding, or damage to fixed fire extinguishing systems, life saving equipment, or bilge pumping systems) will be reported to the Transportation Branch Marine Safety Office, marinesafety@conus.army.mil within 24 hours. The following additional information will be included with the report:

- Time and place of commencement of voyage and destination.

- Direction and force of current.

- Direction and force of wind.

- Visibility in yards.

- Tide and sea conditions.

- Name of person in charge of navigation and names of people on the bridge.

- Name and rank of lookout and where stationed.

- Time when bridge personnel and lookouts were posted on duty.

- Course and speed of watercraft.

- Number of passengers and crew on board.

- Names of passengers and crew.

- Copies of all pertinent log entries.

- List of the witnesses names and addresses.

- Date steering gear and controls were last tested.

- Date and place where compasses were last adjusted and deviation, if any, at the time of the accident.

- Statement of any outside assistance received.

- Diagrams of damage and pertinent documents.

- Photos of damage.

- Any other details not covered above.

COLLATERAL INVESTIGATION REPORTS

11-16. A collateral investigation is required in many cases for Class A, B, or C accidents to record and preserve the facts for litigation, claims, and disciplinary and administrative actions. These investigations are conducted in accordance with AR 15-6. All fatal accidents require a collateral investigation. Those accidents that generate a high degree of public interest or are likely to result in litigation for or against the government also require a collateral investigation.

NOTE: Personnel investigating an accident under AR 385-10 will not be involved in tracking, handling, or reviewing collateral investigations nor will they be involved in establishing collateral investigation procedures.

Appendix A

Essential Elements of Information (EEI)

PORT EEI CHECKLIST

The critical items of information or intelligence required to plan and execute an operation are the essential elements of information (EEI). These elements are developed at the battalion and higher echelons based on mission and situation. EEI are classified according to classification guidance for the operation, and priorities are designated for each item of information. The EEI are then forwarded through intelligence channels for fulfillment. The following EEI lists serve as areas of important items to consider for terminal and beach operations.

NOTE: Port or beach EEI is defined for specific operations. All operations require the use of lines of communication (LOC) EEI and threat EEI. Town EEI is used for all villages, towns, or cities at or near the area of operations.

General:

- Customs regulations.
- Map sheet number (series, sheet, edition, and date).
- Nautical chart number.
- Grid coordinates and longitude/latitude.
- Military port capacity and method of capacity estimation.
- Dangerous or endangered marine or land animals in the area.
- Names, titles, and addresses of port authority and agent personnel.
- Nearest US consul.
- Port regulations.
- Current tariffs.
- Frequencies, channels, and call signs of the port's harbor control.
- Complete description of the terrain within 25 miles of the port.
- Location of nearest towns (see town EEI), airports, and military installations.
- Threat assessment.

Harbor:

- Types of harbor.
- Lengths and location of breakwaters.
- Depth (mean lower low water), length and width in the fairway.
- Current speed and direction in the fairway.

- Size and depth (mean lower low water) of the turning basin.
- Location and description of navigational aids.
- Pilotage procedures required.
- Location and degree of silting.
- Size, frequency, and effectiveness of dredging operations.
- Description of the port's dredger.
- Description of sandbars or reefs in the area.
- Identity of any marine plants that could inhibit movement of ships or lighterage.
- Composition of the harbor bottom (percentage).

Weather and Hydrographic:

- Types of weather conditions encountered in the area.
- Times when these conditions occur.
- Prevailing wind direction per calendar quarter.
- Per calendar quarter, percentage of time for wind speed within 1 to 6 knots, 7 to 16 knots, and over 17 knots.
- Maximum, minimum, and average precipitation per month to the nearest tenth of an inch.
- Maximum, minimum, and average surface air temperature per month.
- Frequency, duration, and density of fog and dust.
- Effects of weather on the terrain.
- Effects of weather on sea vessel travel.
- Effects of weather on logistical operations (such as off-loading materials on vehicles and/or rails).
- Seasonal climatic conditions that would inhibit port operations for prolonged periods (24 hours or more).
- Type and mean range of the tide.
- Direction and speed of the current.
- Minimum and maximum water temperature.
- Per calendar quarter, percentage of time that surf is within 0 to 4 feet, 4 to 6 feet, 6 to 9 feet, and over 9 feet.
- Per calendar quarter, percentage of time that swells are within 0 to 4 feet, 4 to 6 feet, 6 to 9 feet, and over 9 feet.

Anchorages:

- Direction and true bearing from release point (RP) of all anchorages.
- Maximum and minimum depth for each anchorage.
- Current speed and direction at each anchorage.
- Radius of each anchorage.

- Bottom material and holding characteristic of each anchorage.

- Exposure condition of each anchorage.

- Offshore and/or near shore obstacles, what they are, and their distance and true bearing from the port.

Piers:

- Type (wooden, concrete), length and width and present condition of piers located along shoreline.

- Type of location equipment on piers that may be used to off-load cargo.

- Number and types of vessels that piers can accommodate at one time.

- Safe working load level of the pier (in pounds per square foot).

- Water depth (mean lower low water) alongside and leading to the piers.

- Services available (such as water, fuel, and electricity).

- Available pier storage.

- Available maintenance.

- Specialized facilities available for the discharge of RO/RO vessels (such as ramps).

- Height of wharves above mean low water (MLW).

- Current use of wharves.

Cranes:

- Number and location of cranes.

- Characteristics for each crane.

- Type and lift capacity (safe working load in short tons).

- Type of power.

- Dimensions (maximum/minimum radii, outreach beyond wharf face, and above/below wharf hoist).

- Speed (lifting, luffing, and slewing [revolutions]).

- Height and width of port clearance.

- Track length and gauge.

- Make, model, and manufacturer.

- Age and condition.

Other MHE:

- Number, location, and type of MHE on piers that may be used to off-load cargo.

- Type of power.

- Type and Lift capacity (safe working load in short tons).

- Dimensions.

- Make, model, and condition.

- Age and condition.

Stevedores:

- Number and size, efficiency, and working hours of gangs.
- Availability and condition of stevedore gear.
- Arrangements for gangs.
- Availability of other local, national, or third country contract labor.

Harbor Craft:

- Number, type, and location of small craft (tug, pusher, ferry, fishing, pipe-laying, and barges) located in or near the port.
- Characteristics for each craft.
- Size and capacity.
- Number of crew.
- Berthing spaces.
- Number and types of engines.
- Number and types of generators.
- Number of kilowatts for each generator.
- Types of air compressors.
- Number of air compressors.
- Types of engine control (such as mechanized, hydro, and air).
- Location of engine control (wheelhouse, engine room).
- Normal working hours/day of crew.
- Telegraph engine signal, if any.
- Engine manufacturers (Fairbanks, Morse, Detroit, Cooper-Bessemer); types of hull (such as modified V, and round).
- Construction materials (wood, steel, cement, fiberglass).
- Number and types of rudder (steering, flanking).
- Number of propellers (single, twin, or triple).
- Type of radio (AM, FM, and frequency range).
- Layout of the rail and road network in the port.

Storage Facilities:

- Number and location of storage facilities.
- Characteristics of each.
- Product stored.
- Type of storage (open, covered, or refrigerated).

- Capacity and/or dimensions.

- Floor, wall, and roof material.

- State of repair.

- Special facilities.

- Security facilities.

Port Equipment Repair Facilities:

- Location, size, and capabilities of repair facilities.

- Type of equipment.

- Number and ability of repairmen.

- Availability and system of procuring repair parts.

Ship Repair Facilities:

- Number and type of dry dock and repair facilities.

- Quality of work and level of repairs that can be made.

- Location, size, and use of other buildings in the port.

- Height of doorways and internal ceiling height (in feet).

- Method for obtaining potable and boiler water in the port. (NOTE: See town EEI for additional items.)

- Method for obtaining fuel, lube, and diesel oil in the port. (NOTE: See town EEI for additional items.)

- Medical personnel in port. (NOTE: See town EEI for additional items.)

- Electrical generating facilities in port or provisions for obtaining electricity from an external source. (NOTE: See town EEI for additional items.)

- Ship-handling services available in the port.

Security:

- Size and availability of the security force.

- Physical security facilities currently in use at the port (security fences, storage areas, electronic surveillance, and alarms).

- Fire-fighting equipment available.

BEACH EEI CHECKLIST

General:

- Map sheet number (series, sheet, edition, and date).

- Size and availability of the port security force.

- Physical security facilities currently in use at the port (security fences, storage areas, electronic surveillance, and alarms).

- Fire-fighting equipment available in the port.
- Nautical chart number.
- Grid coordinates and longitude and latitude of the center beach (CB), left flank (LF), and right flank (RF).
- Shape, length, and usable length of the beach.
- Firmness of the beach.
- Beach width and backshore width at LF, RF, and points every 200 yards in between.
- Beach composition by percent at the near-shore, foreshore, and backshore.
- Any dangerous or endangered marine or land animals in the area.
- Underwater Obstructions.

Anchorages:

- Direction and true bearing from CB of all anchorages.
- Maximum and minimum depth for each anchorage.
- Current speed and direction at each anchorage.
- Radius of each anchorage.
- Bottom materials and holding characteristics of each anchorage.
- Exposure condition of each anchorage.
- Protected anchorage nearby for landing craft.

Approaches:

- Beach gradient at LF, RF and points every 200 yards in between.
- Offshore and/or near-shore obstacles, what are they, and their distance and true bearing from the CB.
- Sandbars or reefs along the beach.
- Composition by percent of the immediate offshore bottom.
- Description of navigational aids.
- Any marine plants that could inhibit movement of landing craft.

Hydrographic:

- Type and mean range of the tide.
- Direction and speed of the current.
- Minimum and maximum water temperature.
- Per calendar quarter, percentage of time the surf is within 0 to 4 feet, 4 to 6 feet, 6 to 9 feet, and over 9 feet.
- Per calendar quarter, percentage of time that swells are within 0 to 4 feet, 4 to 6 feet, 6 to 9 feet, and over 9 feet.

Weather:

- Types of weather conditions encountered in the area.

- Times when these conditions occur.

- The prevailing wind direction per calendar quarter.

- Per calendar quarter, percentage of time the wind speed is within 1 to 6 knots, 7 to 16 knots, and over 17 knots.

- Maximum, minimum, and average precipitation per month to the nearest tenth of an inch.

- Maximum, minimum and average surface air temperature per month.

- Frequency, duration, and density of fog.

- Effects of weather on terrain, sea vessel travel, and logistical operations (such as offloading materials on vehicles and/or rails).

- Seasonal climatic conditions that would inhibit LOTS operations for prolonged periods (24 hours or more).

Vehicle Trafficability:

- Vehicle trafficability in dry and wet conditions for wheeled and tracked vehicles.

- Type of matting recommended (such as MOMAT or steel planking).

- Exit points for vehicles along the beach.

- Roads along or leading from the beach.

- Materials that make up roads.

- Condition of the roads.

- Distance from the road to MLW and high water line.

Construction:

- Buildings on the beach.

- Distance and true bearing of buildings from CB.

- Size, construction, and use of buildings.

- Fortifications or obstacles on the beach.

- Distance and true bearing of obstacles from the CB.

- Size and construction of fortifications or obstacles.

- Piers along the beach.

- Distance and true bearing of piers from the CB.

- Pier type, length, width, construction material present condition and water depth alongside.

Near Hinterland (within 1,000 meters of the shoreline):

- Dunes along the beach; description of dune length, width, height, and distance from high water shoreline.

- Characteristics of terrain and vegetation.

- Where the tree line begins.

- Availability and description of open storage areas.

- Power and/or pipelines in the area.

- Location size, construction, and purpose of any buildings or other man-made objects.

- Estuaries and inland waterways; distance from high water shoreline (see lines of communication EEI).

- Road and/or rail networks (see lines of communication EEI).

- Town (see town EEI).

Far Hinterland (1 to 30 kilometers from the beach):

- Characteristics of terrain and/or vegetation.

- Power and/or pipelines in the area.

- Road, rail and water networks (see lines of communication EEI).

- Town (see town EEI).

- Nearest airport (airport EEIs are developed when required).

- Military installations in the area and description of each.

LINES OF COMMUNICATION EEI CHECKLIST

Primary and Secondary Roads:

- Type of primary roads (concrete, asphalt).

- Primary and secondary roads that allow north-south and lateral movement.

- Capacity of intra-terminal road networks.

- Present condition of these roads.

- Bridges constructed along these roads.

- Construction materials of bridges along these routes.

- Width and weight allowance of these bridges.

- Overpasses and tunnels located along these routes.

- Width and height allowance of the overpasses and tunnels.

- Major cities that roads enter and exit.

Rail:

- Type of rail line and rail network.

- Location and weight allowance of rail bridges.

- Location and restriction of overpasses and tunnels that pass over rail lines.

- Gauges.

- Equipment available (for example, locomotives [steam or diesel], flatcars, and boxcars).
- Ownership of rail network (private or government).
- Address and telephone number of rail network authorities.

Inland Waterway:

- Nautical/bathometric chart number.
- Width of the waterway.
- Average depth, speed of the water, and shallow point.
- With given cargo weight, how close to the shore will water depth allow types of vehicles.
- Capacity to conduct clearance operations via inland waterway.
- Points at which tugs will be needed to support travel of vessel.
- Points along the coast most suitable for different types of sea and/or land operations.
- Types of channel markers.
- Points most suitable for mining of waterway.
- Effect, such as timely delay, that mining would have on ship passage.
- Locations at which waterways narrow into choke point.
- Prevailing wind direction and average wind speed in knots per calendar quarter.
- Other than choke points, locations where vessels are vulnerable to shore fire.
- Security that is available for vessels (underway, at anchor, or tied up).
- Type of special units, such as water sappers, that can threaten sea vessels.
- Local shore security available to protect vessels once they are docked.
- Type and number of local watercraft available to move cargo.
- Maintenance capability that exists for these vessels.
- Docks along the waterway.
- Local regulations that govern inland waterway operations.
- Address and/or telephone number of the waterway authorities, if any.

THREAT EEI CHECKLIST

- Enemy threat and capability in the area of operation (air, ground, WMD).
- Description of local overt/covert organization from which hostile action can be expected.
- Availability of local assets for security operations.
- In addition to port/LOTS operations, other primary targets in the area (military bases, key industrial activities, political/cultural center).

TOWN EEI CHECKLIST

General:

- Name of towns.
- Grid coordinates and longitude and latitude of the towns.
- Size and significance of the towns.
- Primary means of livelihood for the towns.
- Form of government that exists.
- Description of the local police and/or militia.
- Description of the local fire department and equipment.
- Local laws or customs that will impact on operations in this area.
- Availability of billeting.
- Composition of primary roads (concrete, asphalt, compacted gravel, dirt).

Population:

- Size of the population.
- Racial and religious breakdown of the population.
- Languages spoken.
- Political or activist parties that exist in the town.
- Population attitude (friendly or hostile).

Labor:

Names, addresses, and telephone numbers of contracting agents available with services that may be needed during operations (for example husbanding agents, potable water/boiler water, ship repair, coastal vessels, lighterage, machinist, and skilled/ unskilled labor).

Water:

- Availability of potable water and boiler water.
- Size, location, and condition of water purification or desalinization plants.
- Other sources of water, if any.
- Quantity, quality, method, and rates of delivery.
- Special size connections required, if any.
- Water barges available, if any.
- Water requiring special treatment before use, if any.

Medical Facilities:

- Location, size, capabilities, and standards of local hospitals and other medical facilities.

- Availability of doctors (specialized), nurses, and medical supplies.

- Any local diseases which require special attention or preventive action.

- Overall health and sanitary standards of the towns and surrounding area.

Electricity:

- Location, size (kilowatts), and condition of the power station servicing the area.

- How power station is fueled.

- Location and size of transformer stations.

- Voltage and cycles of the electricity.

- Other sources of electricity in the area, such as large generators.

POL:

- Location and size of wholesale fuel distributors in the area (including type of fuel).

- Location and size of POL storage areas and/or tanks in the area (including type of fuel).

Communications:

- Location and size (kilowatts) of local radio and television stations.

- Address of telephone and/or telex offices.

- Description of domestic telephone service in the area (type, condition, number of lines, switching equipment, and use of landlines or microwave).

This page intentionally left blank.

Appendix B
Army Preposition Stocks (APS)-Afloat Request/Approval Letter Example

DEPARTMENT OF THE ARMY
HEADQUARTERS, EIGHTH UNITED STATES ARMY
UNIT #15236
APO AP 96205-0009

EAGD-SPO-WR

26 Jan 07

MEMORANDUM FOR Office of the Deputy Chief of Staff G4 ATTN: DALO-FPP, United States Army, 500 Army Pentagon, Washington D.C. 20310-0500

SUBJECT: Request Permission for 11th ACR Battalion Task Force, 11th Armored Calvary Regiment to Draw and Exercise APS-4 Brigade Set equipment in Support of Exercise Reception, Staging, Onward Movement, and Integration /Foal Eagle 07.

1. Reception, Stationing, Onward movement and Integration and Foal Eagle (RSOI/FE 07) is a ROK-US Combined Forces Command (CFC), ROK government, simulation driven, OPLAN-oriented command post exercise (CPX) and field training exercise (FTX) conducted annually.

2. IAW AR 710-1 Chapter 6 request authorization for the 11th ACR Battalion Task Force (BN TF), draw APS-4 Brigade Set equipment in support of RSOI/FE 07. Request is for 292 combat and tactical vehicles identified in enclosure. Dates remain classified until 30 days prior to the exercise.

3. 11th ACR BN TF will draw and conduct a joint technical inspection in conjunction with Army Field Support B-North East Asia (AFSB-NEA) and Materiel Support Center-Korea (MSC-K). MSC-K is a military service provider funded by Army Materiel Command to maintain readiness of the Brigade Set. Equipment will be issued at TM 10/20 standards.

4. Upon completion of the JRSOI 07 FTX, 11th ACR BN TF will bring the equipment to TM 10/20 standards and conduct joint technical inspection with AFSB -NEA prior to equipment being accepted back into APS-4 storage. 11th ACR is providing OPTEMPO funding to 11th ACR BN TF.

5. POC for this action is CPT Zakeiba Campbell, Chief, War Reserve Branch, G4, DSN 723-6705, and electronic mail: CampbellZ@korea.army.mil.

BRIAN T. NEWKIRK
COL, GS
Assistant Chief of Staff, G4

Figure B-1. Request for APS Equipment

DEPARTMENT OF THE ARMY
OFFICE OF THE DEPUTY CHIEF OF STAFF, G-4
500 ARMY PENTAGON
WASHINGTON, DC 20310-0500

REPLY TO
ATTENTION OF

DALO-ORC-CA

FEB 1 4 2007

MEMORANDUM FOR HEADQUARTERS, EIGHTH UNITED STATES ARMY, UNIT #15236, APO AP 96205-0009

SUBJECT: Authorization to Draw and Exercise Army Prepositioned Stocks-4 (APS-4) Equipment in Support of Exercise Reception, Staging, Onward Movement, and Integration (RSOI) / Foal Eagle 2007

1. References:

 a. Memorandum, Headquarters, Eighth United States Army, G-4, EAGD-SPO-WR, 26 Jan 07, subject: Request Permission for 11th ACR Battalion Task force, 11th Armored Calvary Regiment to Draw and Exercise APS-4 Brigade Set equipment in Support of Exercise Reception, Staging, Onward Movement, and Integration/Foal Eagle 07.

 b. Memorandum, Headquarters, Eighth United States Army, G-4, EAGD-SPO-WR, 12 Feb 07, subject: Memorandum, Headquarters, Special Operations Command – Korea, J-4, SOCK J-4, 26 Jan 07, subject: Naval Special Warfare Group One (Seal Team 1) Requests Tactical Vehicle Support

c. Memorandum, Headquarters, Special Operations Command – Korea, J-4, SOCK J-4, 26 Jan 07, subject: Naval Special Warfare Group One (Seal Team 1) Requests Tactical Vehicle Support

2. Headquarters, Department of the Army (HQDA) concurs with your request to draw an Infantry company set, an Armor Company set and misc support equipment (total of 296 pieces) from APS-4 in support of Exercise RSOI/Foal Eagle 07 from 15 Mar 07 to 15 Apr 07. (See enclosure for detailed listing of stocks to be issued)

3. US Army Material Command (USAMC) will loan 292 pieces of the APS-4 equipment to the 11th Armored Cavalry Regiment (ACR) Battalion Task Force in TM 10/20 condition. Upon completion of the Exercise, the equipment will be returned to the APS-4 stocks under the control of USAMC IAW AR 750-1 at 10/20 condition or funds MIPR to cover cost of repairs by USAMC.

4. US Army Material Command (USAMC) will also loan four (4) HMMWVs to Headquarters, Special Operations Command, Korea (SOCKOR) in maintenance standard TM 10/20 condition from 15 Mar 07 to 15 Apr 07.

Printed on Recycled Paper

Figure B-2. Authorization Approval

Appendix C

Shipboard Security Measures

The shipboard measures are tailored to assist commanding officers and ship masters in reducing the effect of enemy and other security threats to DOD combatant and non-combatant vessels, including U.S. Army vessels worldwide. The Navy labels all ships that do not actively conduct warfare from the sea as "non-combatant". In this context, the term as used in this Appendix applies to Army watercraft.

SHIPBOARD FPCON LEVELS AND MEASURES

FPCON NORMAL Measures:

NORMAL 1: Brief crew on the port-specific threat, the AT and security plans, and security precautions to be taken while ashore. Ensure all hands are knowledgeable of FPCON requirements and that they understand their role in implementation of these measures.

NORMAL 2: Remind all personnel to be suspicious and inquisitive of strangers, be alert for abandoned parcels or suitcases and for unattended vehicles in the vicinity. Report unusual activities to the Officer of the Watch (OOW), Master, or Mate on watch as applicable.

NORMAL 3: Secure and periodically inspect spaces not in use.

NORMAL 4: Review security plans and keep them available.

NORMAL 5: Review pier and shipboard access control procedures including land and water barriers.

NORMAL 6: Ensure sentries, Officer of the Watch, roving patrols, the quarterdeck watch, and gangway watch have the ability to communicate with one another.

NORMAL 7: Coordinate pier and fleet landing security requirements with collocated forces, and/or husbanding agent. Identify anticipated needs for mutual support and define methods of implementation and communication.

FPCON ALPHA Measures:

ALPHA 1: Muster, arm, and brief security personnel on the threat and rules of engagement. Keep key personnel who may be needed to implement security measures on call.

ALPHA 2: DOD noncombatant ships in a non-U.S. Government controlled port, request husbanding agents to arrange and deploy barriers to keep vehicles away from the ship (100 feet in U.S. ports and 400 feet outside the United States as the minimum standoff distances).

ALPHA 3: (U.S. Navy combatant ship-specific – Army vessel crews may be requested to provide personnel to assist on piers at which they are berthed). Randomly inspect vehicles entering pier.

ALPHA 4: Randomly inspect hand-carried items and packages before they are brought aboard.

ALPHA 5: Regulate shipboard lighting as appropriate to the threat environment.

ALPHA 6: When in a non-U.S. Government controlled port, rig hawse pipe covers and rat guards on lines, cables, and hoses. Consider using an anchor collar.

ALPHA 7: When in a non-U.S. Government controlled port, raise accommodation ladders and ramps when not in use.

ALPHA 8: Increase frequency of security drills.

ALPHA 9: Establish internal and external communications, including connectivity checks with the local operational commander, agencies, and authorities that are expected to provide support, if required.

ALPHA 10: Establish procedures for screening food, mail, water, and other supplies and equipment entering the ship.

FPCON BRAVO Measures:

BRAVO 1: Continue or introduce all measures of lower FPCON level.

BRAVO 2: Set Material Condition YOKE (secure all watertight door and hatches), main deck and below.

BRAVO 3: Consistent with local rules, regulations, and/or any applicable SOFA, post armed pier sentries as necessary as necessary.

BRAVO 4: Restrict vehicle access to the pier. Discontinue parking on the pier. Consistent with local rules, regulations, and/or any applicable SOFA, establish unloading zones and move all containers as far away from the ship as possible (100 feet in the United States, 400 feet outside the United States as the minimum stand-off distance).

BRAVO 5: Consistent with the local rules, regulations, and/or any applicable SOFA, post additional armed watches as necessary. Local threat, environment, and fields of fire should be considered when selecting weapons.

BRAVO 6: Post signs in local language to establish visiting and loitering restrictions.

BRAVO 7: When in a non-U.S. Government controlled port, identify and randomly inspect authorized watercraft, such as workboats, ferries, and commercially rented liberty launches, daily.

BRAVO 8: When in a non-U.S. Government controlled port or anchorage, and using shuttle vessels, direct liberty boats to make a security tour around the ship upon departing from and arriving at the ship, with particular focus on the waterline and under pilings when berthed at a pier.

BRAVO 9: Before allowing visitors aboard, inspect all their hand-carried items and packages. Where available, use baggage scanners and walk-through or handheld metal detectors to screen visitors and their packages prior to boarding the ship.

BRAVO 10: Implement measures to keep unauthorized craft away from the ship. Authorized craft should be carefully controlled. Coordinate with host-nation's husbanding agent or local port authority, as necessary, and request their assistance in controlling unauthorized craft.

BRAVO 11: Raise accommodation ladders, etc., when not in use. Clear ship of all unnecessary stages, camels, barges, oil donuts, and lines.

BRAVO 12: Review liberty policy in light of the threat and revise it as necessary to maintain safety and security of ship and crew.

BRAVO 13: All DOD ships avoid conducting activities that involve gathering a large number of crewmembers at the weather decks. Where possible, relocate such activities inside the skin of the ship.

BRAVO 14: Ensure an up-to-date list of bilingual personnel for the area of operations is readily available. Maintain warning tape, in both the local language and English, in the bridge, pilot house, or quarterdeck, for use on the ship's announcing system to warn small craft to remain clear.

BRAVO 15: If they are not already armed, arm the quarterdeck, gangway or mate on watch.

BRAVO 16: If they are not already armed, consider arming the sounding and security patrol.

BRAVO 17: Review procedures for expedient issue of firearms and ammunition to the shipboard security reaction force (SRF) and other members of the crew, as deemed necessary by the commanding officer/master.

BRAVO 18: Instruct watches to conduct frequent, random searches of the pier, including pilings and access points.

BRAVO 19: Conduct visual inspections of the ship's hull and ship's boats at intermittent intervals and immediately before it is put to sea using both landside personnel and waterside patrols.

BRAVO 20: Hoist ship's boats aboard when not in use.

BRAVO 21: Terminate all public visits. In U.S. Government controlled ports, host visits (family, friends, small groups sponsored by the ship) may continue at the commanding officer's/master's discretion.

BRAVO 22: After working hours, reduce entry points to the ship's interior by securing infrequently used entrances. Safety requirements must be considered.

BRAVO 23: In non-U.S. Government-controlled ports, use only one brow/gangway to access the ship (remove any excess brows/gangways). Very large ships may use two as required, when included in an approved AT Plan specific to that port visit.

BRAVO 24: In non-U.S. Government-controlled ports, maintain the capability to get underway on short notice or as specified by standard operating procedures.

BRAVO 25: In non-U.S. Government-controlled ports, consider the layout of fire hoses. Brief designated crew personnel on procedures for repelling boarders, small boats and ultra-light aircraft.

BRAVO 26: Where applicable, obstruct possible helicopter landing areas.

BRAVO 27: Where possible, monitor local communications (ship-to-ship, TV, radio, police scanners).

BRAVO 28: As appropriate, inform local authorities of actions being taken as FPCON increases.

BRAVO 29: If the threat situation warrants, deploy small boats to conduct patrols in the immediate vicinity of the ship. Brief boat crews and arm them with appropriate weapons considering the threat, the local environment, and fields of fire.

FPCON CHARLIE Measures:

CHARLIE 1: Continue or introduce all measures of lower FPCON levels.

CHARLIE 2: Consider setting Material Condition Zebra (secure all access doors and hatches), main deck and below.

CHARLIE 3: Cancel liberty. Execute emergency recall.

CHARLIE 4: Prepare to get underway on short notice. If conditions warrant, request permission to sortie/get underway.

CHARLIE 5: Block unnecessary vehicle access to the pier.

CHARLIE 6: Coordinate with host-nation husbanding agent and/or local port authorities to establish a small boat exclusion zone around ship.

CHARLIE 7: Deploy the SRF to protect command structure and augment posted watches. Station the SSDF to provide 360-degree coverage of the ship.

CHARLIE 8: Energize radar and/or sonar, rotate screws, and cycle rudder(s) at frequent and irregular intervals, as needed to assist in deterring, detecting, or thwarting attacks.

CHARLIE 9: Consider staffing repair locker(s). Be prepared to staff one repair locker on short notice. Ensure adequate lines of communications are established with damage control central.

CHARLIE 10: If available and feasible, consider use of airborne assets as an observation/FP platform.

CHARLIE 11: If a threat of swimmer attack exists, activate an anti-swimmer watch.

CHARLIE 12: In non-U.S. Government-controlled ports and if unable to get underway, consider requesting armed security augmentation from area Combatant Commander.

FPCON DELTA Measures:

DELTA 1: Fully implement all measures of lower FPCON levels.

DELTA 2: Permit only necessary personnel topside.

DELTA 3: If possible, cancel port visit and get underway.

DELTA 4: Employ all necessary weapons to defend against attack.

Appendix D

Crew Requirements by Platform

Table D-1. Class A2 LSV Detachment

DUTY TITLE	GRADE	SKILL	REQUIRED
Vessel Master	W4	880A2	1
Chief Engineer	W4	881A2	1
Chief Mate	W3	880A2	1
First Assistant Engineer	W3	881A2	1
Mate	W2	880A1	2
Assistant Engineer	W2	881A1	2
Detachment Sergeant (Sr. Navigator)	E7	88K40	1
Marine Maintenance NCO	E7	88L40	1
Boatswain (Navigator)	E6	88K30	1
Junior Marine Engineer (Rover)	E6	88L30	1
Leading Seaman (Navigator)	E5	88K20	1
Senior Marine Engineman	E5	88L20	2
Emergency Care Sergeant	E5	68W20	1
Food Operations SGT	E6	92G30	1
Radio Operator-Maintainer	E4	25C10	1
Seaman	E4	88K10	4
Marine Engineman	E4	88L10	2
Cook	E4	92G10	1
Seaman	E3	88K10	3
Marine Engineman	E3	88L10	2
Cook	E3	92G10	1
Total			**31**

Table D-2. Class A2 Large Tug (LT 128')

DUTY TITLE	GRADE	SKILL	REQUIRED
Vessel Master	W4	880A2	1
Chief Engineer	W4	881A2	1
Chief Mate	W3	880A2	1
First Asst Engineer	W3	881A2	1
Mate	W2	880A1	2
Assistant Engineer	W2	881A1	2
Boatswain	E7	88K40	1
Marine Maintenance NCO	E7	88L40	1
Leading Seaman	E5	88K20	1
Senior Marine Engineman	E5	88L20	1
Emergency Treatment NCO	E5	68W20	1
First Cook	E5	92G20	1
Seaman	E4	88K10	2
Marine Engineman	E4	88L10	2
Seaman	E3	88K10	2
Marine Engineman	E3	88L10	2
Cook	E4	92G10	1
Total			**23**

Table D-3. Class A2 Large Tug (100', FLT III)

DUTY TITLE	GRADE	SKILL	REQUIRED
Vessel Master	W4	880A2	1
Chief Engineer	W4	881A2	1
Mate	W2	880A1	1
Assistant Engineer	W2	881A1	1
Boatswain	E6	88K30	1
Marine Maint Supervisor	E6	88L30	1
Leading Seaman	E5	88K20	1
Senior Marine Engineman	E5	88L20	1
First Cook	E5	92G20	1
Seaman	E4	88K10	2
Marine Engineman	E4	88L10	1
Seaman	E3	88K10	2
Marine Engineman	E3	88L10	1
Cook	E4	92G10	1
Total			**16**

Table D-4. Class A1 Landing Craft Utility (LCU)

DUTY TITLE	GRADE	SKILL	REQUIRED
Vessel Master	W2	880A1	1
Chief Engineer	W2	881A1	1
Mate	E7	88K40	1
Assistant Engineer	E7	88L40	1
Boatswain	E6	88K30	1
Jr Marine Engineer	E6	88L30	1
Leading Seaman	E5	88K20	1
Senior Marine Engineman	E5	88L20	1
Seaman	E4	88K10	1
Marine Engineman	E4	88L10	1
Seaman	E3	88K10	1
Marine Engineman	E3	88L10	1
Cook	E4	92G10	1
Total			**13**

*Note: For voyages of extended duration (see Definitions), add *Emergency Treatment NCO, E5, 68W, 1.*

Table D-5. Class A1 Small Tug (ST)

DUTY TITLE	GRADE	SKILL	REQUIRED
Vessel Master	E7	88K40	1
Chief Engineer	E7	88L40	1
Boatswain	E6	88K30	1
Asst Marine Engineer	E6	88L30	1
Leading Seaman	E5	88K20	1
Seaman	E4	88K10	2
Marine Engineman	E4	88L10	2
Seaman	E3	88K10	1
Marine Engineman	E3	88L10	1
Cook	E5	92G20	1
Total			**12**

Table D-6. Class B Landing Craft Mechanized (LCM) Mod 1

DUTY TITLE	GRADE	SKILL	REQUIRED
Coxswain	E5	88K20	2
Seaman	E4	88K10	1
Marine Engineman	E4	88L10	1
Seaman	E3	88K10	1
Marine Engineman	E3	88L10	1
Total (3 per shift for 24 hour ops)			**6**

Table D-7. Class B Landing Craft Mechanized (LCM) Mod 2

DUTY TITLE	GRADE	SKILL	REQUIRED
Coxswain	E5	88K20	2
Seaman	E4	88K10	1
Senior Marine Engineman	E5	88L20	2
Marine Engineman	E4	88L10	1
Seaman	E3	88K10	1
Marine Engineman	E3	88L10	1
Total (4 per shift for 24 hour ops)			**8**

Table D-8. Class B Causeway Ferry (CF)

DUTY TITLE	GRADE	SKILL	REQUIRED
Marine Ops NCO	E7	88K40	2
Boatswain	E6	88K30	2
Coxswain	E5	88K20	2
Senior Marine Engineman	E5	88L20	2
Seaman	E4	88K10	3
Marine Engineman	E4	88L10	2
Seaman	E3	88K10	3
Total (24 hour ops)			**16**

Table D-9. Class B Floating Causeway (FC) Pier

DUTY TITLE	GRADE	SKILL	REQUIRED
Main Segment:			
Marine Ops NCO	E7	88K40	1
Boatswain	E6	88K30	1
Leading Seaman	E5	88K20	2
Seaman	E4	88K10	6
Senior Forklift Operator	E5	88H20	1
Seaman	E3	88K10	6
RT Forklift Operator	E4	88H10	1
Subtotal Main Segment			*18*
Warping Tug Crew (two Tugs)			
Coxswain	E5	88K20	4
Senior Marine Engineman	E5	88L20	2
Seaman	E4	88K10	6
Marine Engineman	E4	88L10	2
Seaman	E3	88K10	6
Subtotal 2 Warping Tug Crews			*20*
Total for 24 hour ops			**38**

Table D-10. Class B Roll on/Roll off Discharge Platform (RRDF)

DUTY TITLE	GRADE	SKILL	REQUIRED
Main Segment (two crews):			
Marine Ops NCO	E7	88K40	2
Boatswain	E6	88K30	2
Leading Seaman	E5	88K20	4
Senior Forklift Opr	E5	88H20	2
RT Forklift Opr	E4	88H10	2
Seaman	E4	88K10	12
Seaman	E3	88K10	12
Subtotal Main Segment			*36*
Warping Tug Crew (two Tugs)			
Coxswain	E5	88K20	8
Marine Engineman	E4	88L10	4
Seaman	E4	88K10	12
Marine Engineman	E4	88L10	4
Seaman	E3	88K10	12
Subtotal 2 Warping Tug Crews			*40*
Total for 24 hour ops			**76**

Table D-11. Class A1 Barge Derrick, (BD) 115 ton

DUTY TITLE	GRADE	SKILL	REQUIRED
Chief Engineer	W2	881A1	1
Boatswain	E6	88K30	1
Senior Marine Engineman	E5	88L20	1
Seaman	E4	88K10	2
Marine Engineman	E4	88L10	2
Seaman	E3	88K10	2
Marine Engineman	E3	88L10	2
Senior Crane Operator	E5	88H20	1
Crane Operator	E4	88H10	1
Cook	E5	92G20	1
Total for 24 hour ops			**14**

Table D-12. Class C Barge Liquid, (BG)

DUTY TITLE	GRADE	SKILL	REQUIRED
Fuel Handling Spec	E5	92F20	1
Fuel Handling Spec	E4	92F10	1
Seaman	E4	88K10	1
Marine Engineman	E4	88L10	1
Seaman	E3	88K10	1
Marine Engineman	E3	88L10	1
Total for 24 hour ops			**6**

Note: The Joint High Speed Vessel crew composition will be determined based upon operational mission requirements and MARKS.

This page intentionally left blank.

Glossary

This glossary lists acronyms and terms with Army, multi-Service, or joint definitions, and other selected terms. Where the Army and joint definitions are different, *(Army)* follows the term.

AA/AD	Anti access and access denial
AAHSS	Austere Access, high speed sealift
ABCA	American, British, Canadian, Australian (and New Zealand) Armies Program
A/C	air condition
ACP	Allied Communications Publications
ABS	automated battlebook system
ABS	American Bureau of Shipping
ACOM	Army Command
AFRTS	Armed Forces Radio and Television Service
AFSB	Army field support brigade
AKO	Army Knowledge Online
ALT	acquisition, logistics, technology
AMC	Army Materiel Command
AMC/USAMMA	United States Army Medical Materiel Agencey
AO	area of operations
AOR	area of responsibility
APOD	aerial port of debarkation
APOE	aerial port of embarkation
APS	Army pre-positioned stocks
APS	Afloat Prepostioned Stock
AR	Army regulation
ARSTAF	Army staff
ASCC	Army Service component command
ASCM	Antiship Cruise Missile
ASMIS	Army Safety Management Information System
BCOTM	Battle command on the move
BDA	Battle damage assessment
BD	Barge derrick
BG	Barge, liquid cargo, fuel
BLCP	Beach lighterage control point
BRM	Brigade resource management
C2	command and control

CB	Center beach
CF	Causeway ferry
C2	Command and control
CBRN	Chemical, biological, radiological, nuclear
CDE	Chemical detection equipemnt
CEN	Communications, electronics & navigation
C4ISR	Command, control, communications, computers, & intelligence
CRM	Composite risk management
CWIB	Chief of Watercraft Inspection Branch
CCDR	Combatant commander
CCJO	Capstone Concept for Joint Operations
CLASS A	Vessels designed for continuous operation. This class includes the large high speed vessels, large tugboats, logistics
CLASS B	Self-propelled vessels designed for intermittent use or for relatively continuous use in localized areas
CLASS C	Non-self-propelled watercraft. This class inculdes all barges
CMF	Containerized maintenance facility
COCOM	Combatant Command
COMSEC	Communications security
CBM	Condition Based Maintenance
CONUS	Continental United States
COSIS	Care of supplies in storage, maintenance
CP	Command post
COP	Common operational picture
CSP	Causeway section
CSNP	Nonpowered causeway sections
DALO-FPP	Department of Army Logistics-Force Protection Program
DA PAM	Department of the Army pamphlet
DCS	Defense communication systems
DEL	Deployment equipment list
DMS	Defense messaging system
DOD	Department of Defense
DOTMLPF	Doctrine, organizations, training, materiel, leadership, and education, personnel and facilities
DODI	Department of Defense Instruction
DSC	digital selective calling
ECDIS	Electronic chart display information system
ECCM	Electronic communication countermeasures
ECP	entry check point

EoF	escalation of force
EEI	essential element of information
EOOW	Engineering-officer-of-the-watch
ESC	expeditionary sustainment command
FBCB2	Force XXI Battle Command, Brigade and Below
FC	Floating causeway
FLT III	foot large tug
FLO/FLO	float-on/float-off
FM	field manual; financial management
FM	frequency modulated
FMC	financial management center
FORSCOM	United States Army Forces Command
FPCON	Force protetion conditions
FRS	forward repair system
GCC	geographic combatant commander
GMDSS	Global maritime distress and safety system
GPS	Global Poistioning System
HCCC	Harbormaster command & control center
HLVTOL	heavy lift vertical take-off and landing
HMOD	harbormaster operations detachment
HF	high frequencey
HHC	Headquarters and Headquarters Company
HN	host nation
HMOD	harbormaster operation detactment
HNS	host nation support
HQDA	headquarters Department of the Army
HQ	headquarters
HSCDS	high speed craft deck systems
HSCES	high speed craft engineering systems
IAW	in accordance with
IMMC	Inventory Materiel Management Centers
INMARSAT SES	International Maritime Satellite Systems Ship Earth Station
INMARSAT	Internet Sites for thoses vessels with satellite communication capability
IPD	issue priority designtion
ISO	International Organization for Standardization

JAT	Joint anti-terrorism guide
JCIDS	Joint Capabilities Integration and Development System
JCA	Joint capability areas
JCS	Joint Chief of Staff
JFC	joint force commander
JFLCC	joint force land component command
JHSV	joint high speed vessel
JLOTS	Joint logistics over the shore
JLCC	joint lighterage control center
JOA	joint operatiing area
JOE	Joint operating enviroment
JP	joint publication
JTF	joint task force
JTS	Joint training system
LF	left flank
LCM	landing craft mechanized
LCMC	life cycle management command
LCM-8	landing craft mechanized
LCU-2000	landing craft utility
LOC	line of communications
LASH	load aboard ships or heavy lift vessels
LOGMARS	logistics applications of automated making and reading symbology
LO/LO	lift on/ lift off
LOTS	logistics over-the-shore
LSV	logistics support vessel
LT	Large tug (800)
LANDWarNet	Land War Net
LMSR	Large medium speed roll-on/roll-off ships
MAM	Maintance advisory message
MACOM	Major Army Command
MARS	Military affiliated radio stations
MANPADS	Man-portable air defense system
MAC	Maintenanance allocation chart
MCS	maintenance condition survey
MCO	major combat operations
MCS	modular causeway system
MDMP	leaders in military decision making process
MEDEVAC	medical evacuation

METT-TC	Mission, enemy, terrain and weather, troops and support available, time available and civil considerations
MHE	materials handling equipment
MOS	military occupational specialty
MoMAT	mobility matting
MSR	main supply routes
MSC	military sealift command
MSI	modified surf index
MST	maintenance support team
MWD	Military working dog
MWOs	modification work orders
NAP	Not authorized prepositioning
NCO	Non-Commissioned Officer
NCOIC	Non-Commissioned Officer in Charge
NDS	National defense strategy
NM	Nautical miles
NMC	not mission capable
NORTHCOM	Northen Command
NVDs	night vision devices
NDS	national security strategy
OCONUS	outside the continental United States
OCCM	pre-owned condition cyclic maintenance
OPCON	operational control
ORP	Ocean reception point
OSHA	Occupational Safety & Health Administration
PABX	public automatic branch exchange
PD-AWS	Product Director, Army Watercraft System
PFDs	personnel floatation devices
PMCS	Preventive maintenance checks & services
PPR	pre-planned responses
QDR	quadrennial defense review
RF	radio frequency
RFF	request for force
RFID	radio frequency identification
RIC	routing identifier code
ROE	rules of engagement

RO/RO	roll-on/ roll-off
RSOI	reception, staging, onward movement, integration
S-1	personnel staff officer
SAMS	Standard Army Maintenance System
SDDC	Surface Deployment and Distribution Command
SIPRNET	secure internet protocol network
SES	ship earth station
SITREPs	summaries, situation reports
SLCP	ship lighterage control point
SOFA	status-of-forces agreement
SOP	standing operating produres
SOLAS	safety of life at sea, 1974
SOUM	safety of use message
SPOD	seaport of debarkation
SPOE	seaport of embarkation
SSA	supply support activity
STONs	short tons
SSTOL	super short take off and landing
STAMIS	standard Army management information system
SSC	small-scale contingencies
STCW	standard of training, certification, and watch
TADSS	Training aids, devices, simators and simulatioins
TACOM	tank automotive and armaments command
TACON	tactical control
TC	tactical communication
TAMMS	the Army maintenance management system - aviation
TM	technical manual
TOE	table of organization and equipment
TTOE	transportation theater opening element
TTP	tactics, techniques & procedures
TRADOC	United States Army Training and Doctrine Command
TSC	theater sustainment command
TSCP	theater support and cooperation program
USCG	United States Coast Guard
USMC	United States Marine Corps
USTRANSCOM	United States Transportation Command
UUV	Unmmanned under sea vehicles

VHF	Verg high frequencey
VSO	vessel support office
WNMP	Watercraft National Maintenance Point
WFMC	Watercraft field maintenance company
WIB	Watercraft Inspection Branch
WT	warping tug

SECTION II DEFINITIONS

alliance

The relationship that results from a formal agreement (such as a treaty) between two or more nations for broad, long-term objectives that further the common interests of the members (see JP 3-0).

anticipation

The ability to foresee events and requirements and initiate necessary actions that most appropriately satisfy a response.

Army Field Support Brigade (AFSB)

An organization which provides integrated and synchronized acquisition logistics and technology (ALT) support, less medical, to Army operational forces. (FM 4-93.41)

Atoll reefs

These barrier reefs enclose lagoons. They usually have a crescent shape with the convex side toward the sea. They may contain reef islands, or heads, composed of accumulated debris from the reef.

Barrier Reefs

Barrier reefs lie offshore and are separated from the land by a lagoon. There may be a fringing reef on the land side of the barrier reef.

battle command

The art and science of understanding, visualizing, describing, directing, leading, and assessing forces to impose the commander's will on a hostile, thinking, and adaptive enemy. Battle command applies.

Boatswain

The boatswain is responsible for maintenance and reporting operational conditions of the deck department machinery and equipment. In additions, the boatswain is responsible for the conduct, discipline, and direct supervision of deck personnel. The boatswain also supervises preparation of the vessel for sea, and cargo or towing operations and stands underway watch as appropriate.

Bridge-to-Bridge Radiotelephone

Commonly called bridge-to-bridge, this Very High Frequency (VHF) radiotelephone is part of the GMDSS requirement, and is designed to communicate between ships and from ship to shore.

Chief Engineer

The chief engineer is responsible to the master for the efficient, safe, and economical operation of the engine department. Duties include maintaining vessel maintenance logs, records, reports and inventory of repair parts. Additionally, the chief engineer directs & supervises maintenance and repair of vessel equipment in accordance with AR 750-1 and Maintenance Allocation Chart (MAC).

Chief Mate

The chief mate serves as assistant to the master The chief mate is responsible for all deck operations and maintenance of deck department equipment. When required, the chief mate also navigates the vessel during appropriate watches.

condition based management

The use of CBM is a transformational change in the scheduling, performance, management and, more importantly, the impact of maintenance on readiness and combat power.

Crane Operator

The crane operator operates the barge crane in support of lift operations, as directed. This position requires familiarization with emergency station bill and participation in all vessel drills and emergencies.

Cook

The cook prepares and serves two to three meals daily while underway, as directed. This position requires familiarization with emergency station bill and participation in all vessel drills and emergencies.

Coxswain

The coxswain is the master on Class B Vessels and responsible for all aspects of vessel operations.

Detachment Sergeant

The detachment sergeant is responsible to the Master for the training, safety, and good conduct of the Detachment enlisted personnel. When required, the detachment sergeant maintains qualifications for underway watch and stands watch.

Digital Selective Calling (DSC)

The Digital Selective Calling (DSC) capability is the primary capability within GMDSS, and provides the latest technology to Army watercraft communications. It adds an additional capability to the bridge-to-bridge radiotelephone.

Emergency Care Sergeant

The emergency care sergeant is responsible to the master for recording all medical emergencies and provision of emergency medical care of all crew and passengers. Duties include providing emergency treatment for injuries, cardiopulmonary resuscitation, ensures surgical instruments and medical supplies are maintained onboard.

First Assistant Engineer

As assistant to the chief engineer, the first assistant engineer supervises the engine department, to include engine personnel training, safety, maintenance and general ship's business. Additionally, he stands underway watch as Engineering-Officer-of-the-Watch (EOOW).

Fringing reefs

Fringing reefs that are attached to the land. The reef may be only a few feet wide and is seldom more than a mile wide. Inshore vessel channels are often present on fringing reefs, but they do not occur when the reef is narrow and exposed to heavy surf action.

Food Service Sergeant

The food service sergeant operates the ship's galley and is responsible for maintenance of food preparation equipment and area, food preparation, ensuring food handlers' personal hygiene, preparing requests for rations, coordinating ration delivery, and menu preparation. The first cook also prepares and serves meals.

Harbormaster operations

The Harbormaster Detachment is responsible for the coordinating and synchronizing vessel operations and proper functioning of the vessel. Usually, the Harbormaster Detachment goes ashore in one of the first vessels scheduled to land.

High-Frequency Radio Systems

The high-frequency (HF) systems give Army vessels the capability to communicate over great distances. They can be used in both secure and non-secure modes. There are several HF capabilities required, to support the missions of Army watercraft today.

Individual Self-Defense

Commanders have the obligation to ensure that individuals within their respective units are trained on and understand when and how to use force in self-defense.

Joint Forces Commander

The flexibility to tactically position and support the joint operational scheme of maneuver, with unprecedented speed and magnitude.

Large medium speed roll-on/roll-off ships

It is also ideally suited for the discharge or back load of sealift, including Roll-On/Roll-Off (RO/RO) vessels, such as a large medium-speed.

Marine Operations NCO

As the Non-Commissioned Officer In Charge (NCOIC), the marine operations NCO is responsible for all aspects of Modular Causeway System operations.

Marine Maintenance NCO

The marine maintenance NCO is the section sergeant for the engineering department and stands underway watch as Engineer NCOIC of the Watch when required.

Non-Lethal Weapons (NLW) Definition

Non-Lethal Weapons are defined as "Weapons, devices and munitions that are explicitly designed and primarily employed to immediately incapacitate targeted personnel or materiel, while minimizing fatalities, permanent injury to personnel, and undesired damage to property in the targeted area or environment.

Petroleum Specialist

The petroleum specialist conducts watercraft fueling operations in accordance with regulation. This position requires familiarization with emergency station bill and participation in all vessel drills and emergencies.

Radio Operator/Maintainer

The radio operator/maintainer assists in operating and maintaining the vessel's communications equipment and stands underway watch as Radio Operator. This position requires familiarization with emergency station bill and participation in all vessel drills and emergencies.

Seaman

The seaman assists the Boatswain in maintaining and operating all equipment and in the conduct of cargo on load and deck offload operations. Other duties include standing underway watch as helmsman and lookout when required.

Senior Forklift Operator

The senior forklift operator is responsible for operating and maintaining various types of forklifts in support of Modular Causeway System (MCS) operations. This position requires familiarization with emergency station bill and participation in all vessel drills and emergencies.

Senior Radio Operator/Maintainer

The senior radio operator/maintainer is responsible for operating and maintaining the vessel's communications equipment. He also stands underway watch as radio operator. This position requires familiarization with emergency station bill and participation in all vessel drills and emergencies.

Skegs

Stenward extension of the keel of boats and ships which a rudder mounted on the center line.

Transportation Theater Opening Element

The Transportation Theater Opening Element (TTOE) provides guidance on vessel operations at Echelons above Brigade. The plans must be sufficiently detailed so the subordinate units will not have to prepare extensive operation orders.

Unit self defense

A unit commander has the authority and obligation to use all necessary means available and to take all appropriate actions to defend the unit, including elements and personnel, or other US forces in the vicinity, against a hostile act or demonstrated hostile intent.

References

SOURCES USED

These are the sources quoted or paraphrased in this publication. These sources contain relevant supplemental information.

Army Publications

AR 55-355, *Transportation and Travel - Traffic Management Regulations,* 16 February 1995.

FM 5-125, *Rigging Techniques, Procedures, and Applications,* 3 October 1995.

FM 55-9, *Unit Air Movement Planning,* 5 April 1993.

FM 55-50, *Army Water Transport Operations.* 30 September 1993.

FM 55-60, *Army Terminal Operations,* 15 April 1996.

FM 55-450-2, *Army Helicopter Internal Load Operation,.* 5 June 1992.

TM 5-725, *Rigging,* 3 October 1968.

TM 38-250, *Preparing Hazardous Materials for Military Air Shipments (AFJM 24-204; NAVSUP Pub 505; MCO P4030.19G; DLAI 4145.3),* 1 March 1997.

TM 55-601, *Railcar Loading Procedures,* 11 August 1971.

TM 55-607, *Loading and Stowage of Military Ammunition and Explosives aboard Break-bulk Merchant Ships (NAVSEA OP 3221 Rev 2),* 27 December 1988.

TM 55-2200-001-12, *Transportability Guidance for Application of Blocking, Bracing and Tiedown Materials for Rail Transport,* 31 May 1978.

Department of Defense Publications

DOD Regulation 4500.9-R, Part II, *Department of Defense Transportation Regulation (Cargo Movement),* 1 December 2000.

DOD Regulation 4500.9-R, Part III, *Department of Defense Transportation Regulation (Mobility),* 1 November 2001.

Other Publications

AMC Pamphlet 36-1, *Training, AMC Affiliation Program Airlift Planners Course,* 15 March 1995.

CFR 46, *Shipping,* 1 October 2010.

CFR 49, *Transportation,* 1 October 2010.

MIL-STD-12 w/ Change 4, *Military Marking for Shipment and Storage,* 19 September 2007.

SDDCTEA Pamphlet 55-19, *Transportation and Travel, Tiedown Handbook for Rail Movements (Sixth Edition),* September 2003.

SDDCTEA Pamphlet 700-6, *Large, Medium-Speed, Roll-On/Roll-Off Ships Users' Manual,* September 2002.

Army Forms

DA Forms are available on the Army Publishing Directorate web site (www.apd.army.mil).

DA Form 2028, *(Recommended Changes to Publications and Blank Forms)*

DA Form 285, *(Technical Report of United States Army Ground)*

Department of Defense Forms

DD Forms are available from the OSD web site (http://www.dtic.mil/whs/directives/infomgt/forms/index.htm)

DD Form 1384, *(Transportation Control and Movement Document)*

This page intentionally left blank.

Index

This page intentionally left blank.

By order of the Secretary of the Army:

GEORGE W. CASEY
General, United States Army
Chief of Staff

Official:

JOYCE E. MORROW
Administrative Assistant to the
Secretary of the Army
1029206

DISTRIBUTION:

Active Army, Army National Guard, and United States Army Reserve: Not to be distributed; electronic media only.

PIN: 100515-000